D0744184

A FRENCH MODERNIST LIBRARY

Series Editors:
Mary Ann Caws
Richard Howard
Patricia Terry

THE ADVENTURES OF TELEMACHUS

Les Aventures de Télémaque

Translated and with an

introduction by

Renée Riese Hubert &

Judd D. Hubert

University of Nebraska Press

Lincoln & London

THE ADVENTURES

OF

TELEMACHUS

BY

LOUIS ARAGON

Copyright © 1988 by
the University of Nebraska Press
All rights reserved
Manufactured in the United States
of America
Translated from *Les Aven-
tures de Télémaque*,
© Éditions Gallimard, 1966
The translation of
this volume was assisted by a
grant from the
Ministry of Culture of France.
The paper in this book
meets the minimum requirements
of American National
Standard for Information Sciences –
Permanence of Paper
for Printed Library Materials,
ANSI Z39.48-1984.

Library of Congress
Cataloging in Publication Data
Aragon, 1897–1982
The adventures of Telemachus =
(Les aventures de Télémaque)
(A French modernist library)
Translation of:
Les aventures de Télémaque.
1. Telemachus
(Greek mythology)–Fiction.
I. Hubert, Renée Riese, 1916–
II. Hubert, Judd David, 1917–
III. Title.   IV. Series.
PQ2601.R2A9513   1988
843'.912   87-18208
ISBN 0-8032-1021-3
(alkaline paper)

INTRODUCTION

Les Aventures de Télémaque (1922) preceded such major surrealist works as André Breton's *Manifeste du surréalisme* (1924), *Nadja* (1928), *Le Révolver à cheveux blancs* (1932), not to mention Aragon's masterpiece, *Le Paysan de Paris* (1924). Published the same year as Paul Eluard and Max Ernst's collaborative works *Répétitions* and *Les Malheurs des immortels*, it shares with them many of the features that characterize dadaism and that Aragon himself had already displayed in *Anicet ou le panorama* (1921).

Aragon boldly selected the plot and title of Fénelon's

didactic prose epic, not, of course, to express unreserved admiration for this uplifting classic, composed by an archbishop who consistently but daringly moralized history while leaving himself open to parody.[1] In the same way that Ernst (mis)treated Raphael in *Après nous la maternité* (1927), Dali a renaissance virgin in his *Alice in Wonderland* illustrations (1969), Eluard and Péret proverbs in their *152 Proverbes mis au goût du jour* (1925), so did Aragon parody Fénelon. As the surrealists after 1924 emphasized automatic writing, they tended to neglect the highly sophisticated techniques of their earlier creations. Fénelon's *Aventures de Télémaque* provided a remarkably fertile ground for parody because of its boundless intertextuality. In rewriting Homer and Virgil for pedagogical reasons, he had maintained the continuity of the classical tradition while deviating from it mainly in his handling of poetic prose and his not too veiled attack on that warrior king, Louis XIV. The seventeenth-century *Télémaque*, which immediately became a highly controversial bestseller, elicited within a single year two thick volumes of hostile criticism. Aragon's version provides an aggressive *mise en abîme* of the manifold literary conventions of epic literature: heroic models, narrativity, description, and didacticism.[2]

1. See Pierre Carlet de Marivaux, *Le Télemaque travesti*, 2 vols. (Amsterdam: Ryckhoff, 1726).

2. For the criticism hostile to the seventeenth-century *Télémaque*, see Pierre Valentin Faydit, *La Télémacomanie* (Eleutherople: [Paris],

Aragon, who at first remains close to his model, gradually moves from pastiche to parody before striking out on his own to produce a counter-novel of which Fénelon had provided no more than a cast of characters. Aragon did not have to liberate his mind through automatic exercises; but by mastering and playing with the narrative devices of classical episodic fiction he succeeded in freeing himself from the constraints of mimeticism in regard to fable, meaning, and language. One of the striking differences between the opening chapters of the two works relates to the problem of identity. When the classical Telemachus reaches the shores of Calypso's island, his heroic deeds are already inscribed in his youthful features. Because he is Ulysses' son, his identity and fate are fully programmed; through the educational process provided by Mentor, Telemachus cannot help but evolve into the worthy son of the great Odysseus. Aragon deliberately collapses all vestiges of identity and of a progressive initiation into ethical and political righteousness. His pro-

---

1700). Nicolas Gueudeville published four volumes of criticism, *Critique*—about 855 pages!—between 1700 and 1702, at Amsterdam (the listed place of publication, Cologne, is spurious).

Mise-en-abîme (or *abyme*) is a heraldic term, first used critically by André Gide, designating a text that reflects the entire work in which it is inscribed. In graphic terms, the representation within a representation on the Quaker Oats box (the Quaker holding a box of Quaker oats with a picture of a Quaker holding a like box, ad infinitum) is an example of a *mise-en-abîme*.

tagonist by remaining undefined can at best objectify chance. Within one and the same paragraph, he utters these two sentences: "Everything that is myself is incomprehensible" (p. 28); "Everything that is not myself is incomprehensible" (p. 27). Thus Aragon dramatizes an aporic paradox, whereas Fénelon pursues a repetitive path toward godliness. Moreover, Aragon exploits doubt and contradiction, alternating between intense enthusiasm and dadaist derision. In this manner, Fénelon's logic and reason make way for a fertile confusion of textual contradictions and metaphorical unravelings. Throughout, the dadaist unprompted changes and reversals emerge and multiply as though to discourage all assertions of identity in relation to God, ancestors, and society: "Now, the one person in the world about whom I can have no psychological assurance is myself. . . . I ignore what governs me, what continuous change allows others to recognize me and call me by my name. I cannot see myself in profile. At every moment I betray, . . . contradict myself" (p. 50). These words, recited on stage by one of the performing water sprites in the presence of Telemachus, Calypso, Neptune, Mentor, and Eucharis, express the perplexity of all concerned. Significantly, this show, entitled *The Adventures of Telemachus*, takes place at a locality named False Rocks.

Aragon gradually strips Fénelon's characters of an identity inherited from myths and past literary traditions. Any distinction between mortal and immortal is promptly abolished. Thus Calypso shows herself "unmindful in her sorrow of her immortal self" (p. 11). Later, mortality and immortality will both be cast into the same sea. As in Fénelon's tale, Mentor displaces his immortality as he appears not as youthful Minerva but as an elderly tutor whose hair blackens as soon as he catches sight of Calypso. The shifting of his disguise forces him to resort to lies. His miraculous powers—he suddenly fills the sky with sun—and the ruses by which he attains his ends and repeatedly aids the perpetually threatened and shipwrecked Telemachus appear as eruptions of the immortal self into a mortal performance. In *Les Malheurs des immortels,* Ernst and Eluard, by different devices, had revealed the human foibles of the divinities; Nadja, Breton's heroine, is endowed with visionary intuitions that enable her to communicate with fairies. Mentor manifests his dual presence by gesture and especially by words. In the early stages of the novel he preaches to his pupil and eagerly plays the part of pedant. He pretends to believe in authority, in the family, in responsibility, and to take seriously all the weighted wisdom the dadaists sought to discard: "Why complain about phenomena only to fall prey to pain or pleasure?" (p. 15). "Watch out for the tales of desire,—our own or the other's, for we can hardly tell where lurks the greater danger" (p. 16). His following speech, well rehearsed and full of eloquent exhortations, attracts flocks of gulls and penguins. His poetically worded, philosophically grounded rhetoric, while claiming that "God's work is beautiful, a fit subject for ecstasy" (p. 31), actually formulates a barely disguised invitation to destruction and suicide. The reader is prepared to listen without resistance to the promulgation of the Dd system, which reduces to the same level all words and all actions, including life and death.

Once the novel has acquired sufficient momentum to break the mold borrowed from Fénelon, Mentor explicates and recommends to his pupil the Dd system. This does not mean that the masked goddess has taken on a new identity or switched ideological directions between the first and the second chapter. Identity, as we might suspect, constitutes a false issue, especially for a disguised Minerva expatiating on dadaist destructiveness. The self can no longer be approached from either an analytical or a psychological standpoint. Mentor, who had initially practiced an orderly and structured discourse, replete with relevant questions and submissive answers, soon moves on to a far more challenging and liberating kind of eloquence. In his coherent exposition of the Dd system he borrows from a wide variety of genres and styles: poetic invocations, ads, proverbs, threats, insults, endearments. He delivers each of his messages in fittingly parodic jargons, reiterating deliberate splits between signifier and signified. Far from reflecting the coherent identity of a speaker, language blazes the trail to anarchy.

As Mentor formulates the concepts and techniques of the Dd system, contradictions, paradoxes, and reversals multiply for the sole purpose of self-destruction. His discourse, entailing the sardonic detachment rather than the involvement of the speaker, puts doubt and faith on precisely the same footing. At times he throws language itself into a state of anarchy by heaping together syntactically unrelated words: "Aunt Sally, bowling, knives, roulette, hobby horses, rhetoric, politics, poems, religions, loves, auction bridge" (p. 33). The Dd system provokes unrestrained associations capable of undermining all human activities together with such reliable operations of the cosmos as the succession of night and day.

By focusing on Mentor, we have been led to negate rather than affirm the question and even the principle of identity. We have had to dwell on unexpected shifts, discontinuities, questionable gestures, and perverse activities that verbal prowess will somehow manage to condone or cover up. Telemachus will, we hope, provide us with a more fitting subject for the study of identity and even ground this concept historically in the cleavage between dadaism and surrealism. Because of its alleged durability, identity did not concern the dadaists, always eager to isolate the present moment, the here and now. They differed in this respect from the surrealists, who tended to raise, after the fashion of Breton in *Nadja*, the fundamental question, Who am I? in the hope of ultimately discovering a convulsive identity, a self that reacts to mysterious stimuli and constantly reshapes itself in the presence of another, enigmatically acting as agent.

Like Gide's Nathanaël, Telemachus doggedly departs on his quest for identity and self-discovery; but he follows a far more deceptive course than that of his intertextual cousin.[3] Far from deferring to his tutor by making skillful use of masks and fibs, he succumbs to illusions, for instance in deliberately following his father's traces. Far from returning in Mentor's company to Ithaca, he rushes from one shipwreck and one amorous entanglement to the next. In his experiences on the island, illusion invariably triumphs. He is forced to listen to story after story and tale within tale. Calypso and Eucharis add their favorite narratives, their own alluring textuality to those of others. They merely seek to prevent a departure tantamount to a curtailment of sex. Telemachus encounters nothing but puzzles in seeking clarity or transparency, and he is unable to decipher the codes of his own destiny, which for lack of a better explanation he equates with chance. He has idled his time away in banquets and performances, for his hostess is never sparing in entertainment. In the end he refuses to return to his native land because he no longer feels that he belongs in the real world.

We cannot circumscribe Telemachus's identity by summarizing his adventures. At every step his course links up with some mystery or enigma. As in several sur-

3. Telemachus's quest repeats in parodic form some of the concerns of André Gide's Nathanaël in *Les Nourritures terrestres*, published in 1897.

realist texts, it is hoped that his encounter with the *other* will lead to some form of fulfillment whereby constraining barriers will dwindle and the world beyond will yield all its riches. But it will take more than oracles or Mentor's miracles to solve the riddle of a young man's identity. Texts sealed in glass bottles, far from revealing life's—and Telemachus's—secrets, frustrate any hope the reader may entertain of fictional closure. Even when Mentor reads aloud their contorted lettering, total obscurity stubbornly prevails. The first of the messages emerging from the abyss relates to the loss of sense in regard to space and time, to the inability of the scribe to situate himself in the world. He has merely experienced with the utmost intensity Telemachus's preordained fate—disorientation: "The beatings of my pulse do not inform me any better; their irregularity may result from my incapacity to appreciate any kind of equality in the midst of this appalling nature" (p. 58).

As in Mentor's comments on his system, language in the first message shifts from one type of discourse to another, from the abstrusely metaphysical to the banal, from journalistic reports to poetic flights. Although the rhetoric of the second message hardly seems to lack clarity in explaining an attempt to establish interplanetary communication, Telemachus claims to understand it even less than the first. The third message translates mystery into verbal discontinuity. Here, all discourses merge in a sequence of meaninglessly fragmented narratives, descriptions, announcements, exclamations. To a certain extent this discourse echoes—concretely as well as figuratively—Mentor's rhetorical exposition of the Dd system; and by its verbal traces it resembles Telemachus's peregrinations: "Wheel write the goal later, waved handkerchief I wait: navigators begone" (p. 65). Telemachus's endless repetitions of Eucharis's name provides the opposite type of discourse; it is the direct expression of a desire intensified by reiteration and of an embrace that will prolong itself in the birth of a son.

Contact with nature and with others stimulates exchanges, brings forth metamorphoses, generates unexpected analogies; it becomes difficult to view Telemachus in isolation and as a completely autonomous self. Definitions or other forms of stabilization elude the reader. Unlike the masked Mentor, Telemachus on more than one occasion stands naked; but Aragon undercuts our hope of understanding his protagonist by stating that he is a youth in search of himself "throughout the world." Descent into the self fails to provide the goal of his journey. But can we consider Calypso and Eucharis the high points in his journey or do they merely occasion dreams propitious to surrealist transgressions? "Of all Calypso's nymphs, the most disturbing was Eucharis, so like the milk flowers that Telemachus would sometimes see in his dreams" (p. 25). By their embrace, voluptuous rather than passionate, they become oblivious of the limits imposed by their bodies; their hair becomes almost undistinguishable from the ocean waves; Telemachus feels as heavy as a rock. Thus is the flux of dream imagery set in motion. Familiar contours dissolve; tranformations no longer relate to a fixed center. Nevertheless, between Eucharis and Telemachus a feeling of reciprocity never arises. Eucharis proffers her name like a gift of transparent syllables drained of all mystery. The hero senses in the seashell and in its rumor his own convoluted being. He proclaims his lack of comprehension: "In my left waistcoat pocket I carry a most faithful likeness of myself: a burnished steel watch. It speaks, indicates time and does not understand anything about it" (p. 27). Time, meaning motion and escape, fails to provide a reliable measure for unfolding; with its ever changing rhythms it manifests itself by the same sort of dispersion and fragmentation that characterize its owner: ". . . while their hair vanished in the clouds; here and there the ground split open to the level of precious mines from which flashed forth the landscape light" (p. 14).

Refractions and reflections prevail throughout a novel in which mirrors, both black and white, together with luminous shadowy figures multiply and ultimately intertwine. The labyrinth takes on meanings in more than one context; and Narcissus who confused self-love with love for others and mistook illusion for reality, is evoked in the final pages. The lure of unknown depths, haunted by strange, anthropomorphic flora and fauna, leads to other appearances capable of overshadowing or eclipsing reality. The evanescent self reduced to constant flux belongs to a universe where the disguised Minerva proclaims that every successful adventure requires rules and lies. Necessary and deliberate confusion had reduced the city of Troy in all its glory to mere appearance.

Telemachus seeks an identity, but his goal takes the shape of a labyrinthine spiral. Its various twists, its fragmented arches, its unfathomable depths constitute a *mise en abîme* that undoubtedly can be considered more akin to surrealism than to dadaism. We might think of Michel Leiris's infinite repetitions of the woman pictured on the box in *L'Age d'homme* (1946), or Dali's *Suburbs of the Paranoiac-Critical Town* (1936). Telemachus's voyage repeats with unexpected variations the *Odyssey;* his path periodically crosses and distances itself from that of his father. The young man's life, hovering among many episodes, belongs both to chance and to destiny; it bridges contradictions and paradoxes ultimately reducible to a single trace. Calypso and Eucharis, constantly on the threshold of love and desire, will cease to be rivals; they become lesbian reflections of one another through their newly discovered intimacy and will henceforth extend the network of erotic illusion and reversal, which may have been initiated by a transvestite Minerva.

As we can gather from the following description of illusory space—"Then the festivities began: everything that roams the world of imagination, the deserted world of unutilized spaces. . . . the vast world of glances with

the rank germinations of poplars covered by snowy blasts
. . . dashed . . . into the showroom. . . ." (p. 83)—this
particular occasion has nothing special about it, for it
merely sums up many imagined events in which some
unusual or unexpected arrival provides a break in every-
day existence. Telemachus's shipwreck on the island
offers such an occasion: food, songs, seductive whispers,
libidinous gowns. His physical well-being becomes the
focus of everyone's attention. Later, when he descends
into the realm of Neptune, still other creatures provide
him with caring attention and lull him with their dances
into an undersea dream world. His eyes dwell upon corals, upon shells and hypocamps, while he ponders their
miraculous growth and intertwining.

These *mises en abîme* simulate a universe of ever new,
ever changeable affinities that blur all classifications and
distinctions. They undermine the notion of identity since
they foster bold metamorphoses such as the transforma-
tion of urine into coral. These *mises en abîme,* these reflections, are countered by the denials formulated in the
Dd system, which produces its own ramifications and its
own sometimes explosive echoes. It would be tempting
to subsume each one of these divergent manifestations
under a dadaist or a surrealist heading; but we must not
overlook the fact that almost all surrealist texts display
metacritical tendencies and that they invariably function
polemically as well as poetically. As Mentor equates belief
and disbelief, doubt and faith, as he eagerly attempts to

read and decipher the messages emerging from the bottom of the sea, his Dd system is assailed in many ways by other textual and verbal devices.

Such *mises en abîme* are propagated and perhaps ultimately brought to a state of (in)coherence by accompanying spectacles. As we have already suggested, every occasion is turned into a ritual, into a form of entertainment. The masked Minerva seems to be merely one step ahead of the rest of the cast in regard to performance, to the stimulation of illusion. The most important events take place at False Rocks, thus pointing to the illusory quality of the so-called stage itself. But where can opera, dance, calculated gestures, and disguise bring us? False rocks does not prevent the killing of the immortal Minerva by a rock: "No sooner had he finished his speech than a tottering rock broke from the top of the slope and crushed, like an ordinary mortal, the goddess Minerva who had so playfully assumed the shape of an old man and who, thanks to this whim, managed to lose at the same moment her human and her divine existence" (p. 101). And all along Mentor had played, in both meanings of the term. The play or game will end as soon as it can dispose of the player. Mentor had repeatedly advocated play, which in view of the structure of the novel functions both as game and as performance. But does anything exist outside the game, outside performance? Whenever Mentor and Telemachus converse as tutor and disciple, the former's speeches are presented as well-rehearsed exercises in eloquence. But when Mentor explains his Dd system he does not follow a particular mode of discourse, but provides, as we have stated, samples, intertexts, bits of speeches that belong to different codes, different ways of communicating words to an audience; and he assumes at least implicitly several roles. Calypso cannot enjoy moments of intimacy with Mentor without providing a spectacle for a voyeuristic Telemachus.

Everything in the tale leads to the final Homeric laughter of God which convulses whatever may have struck the reader as tragic in the triple death and turns the entire performance into nothing but a sideshow. Through laughter, destiny and chance, meaning and absurdity become equivalent if not synonymous. Although laughter functions as the supreme leveler, particularly in the parodic reversal of Genesis that ends the novel, it belongs primarily to the theater, where it so often provides the sincerest form of applause. It punctuates the frequently humorous novel, distances the characters, and creates gaps where love must perish. Laughter undercuts emotion as it prepares the reader by means of discontinuous reverberations for the final outburst. God, in abeyance until this moment, suggests that he controls suicide no less than escapism. Fénelon's Catholic version of classical heroism can at best provide an intertext in a mock epic used as a vehicle for the reductive efforts of dadaism. Even the emphasis on gratuity that Mentor, an avid reader of Gide, has reiterated throughout the novel may have been counterproductive or reversible. If Mentor and Telemachus had survived, God—no other than the author—would have had to indulge in further subversions in order to prolong their trip.

As Mentor states, "One word is just as good as the next; all of them are ciphers" (p. 21), it follows that words must come to an end even if their mystery lingers on. Whatever Mentor and Telemachus may have represented continues to thrive throughout nature. Their presence is as (un)fulfilling as their absence. Proverbs, sayings, messages are all in a sense gratuitous when it comes to fictional discourse. They undermine their practical function in order to become *other*. They paradoxically merge after the fashion of intertexts into a dadaist discourse exemplified by the third sealed message. But the Delphic oracle, the classical tradition, and surrealist words that make love are all embroiled in the origin and survival of language. When dadaist reversals have sapped conventions, when laughter has become both a primal language and sophisticated metacriticism, only then can the surrealist credo come into being: throughout *The Adventures of Telemachus* language alone can provide a surrealist dynamics.

Indeed, the self, repeatedly shipwrecked in a sea of discourse, dubiously emerges during brief moments of exchange with the other. The contradictory sentences quoted at the beginning go way beyond simple defiance in regard to definition and classification, for their juxtaposition suffices to eliminate all barriers between the self and the world. As Telemachus finds himself alternatively in the arms of the goddess Calypso and of the nymph Eucharis, his self-discovery has little to do with lifelong commitment.

Aragon states in his "Due Apology": ". . . the reader will recognize that throughout the book I have used the word 'love' as a cover for a multiplicity of elements by no means essential to love itself." Love consists first of all of sensual and erotic moments by which Aragon undercuts Fénelon's G-rated brand of sensuousness, invariably subservient to proper esthetic codes and systems. Moreover, Aragon's sensuality belongs to a world governed by desire, by unconscious impulses affirming both life and death. The embrace during which the lover enjoys awareness of self does not remain a private act hidden in a symbolic cave, for it marks an intrusion of the world, capable of making even more problematic than ever the experience of the self. Mirrors function less as physically distancing objects than as a self-reflective power repeatedly staging the interplay of self-fulfillment and desire within an appropriate setting: grotto or seascape.

Concerned merely with desire, none of Aragon's characters would dare consider love a form of duty or possession. Throughout the text appear words referring to masks, disguises, and deceptions, terms that also occur in Fénelon's work. The seventeenth-century writer pointed to a system of false relations between the weak and the strong; he rejected the current code that places man in a state of limitation and servitude. Aragon on the contrary focuses on the illusory nature of human experience in order to question that staged belief in the reality of fiction exploited by his contemporaries. Here we may argue that, at least implicitly, he anticipates Breton's opposition to the dominant type of novel, for not only does he attack the physical reality of the world and the misplaced urge to imitate it, but he insists on the impact of language as a system of signifiers. Capable of displacing relationships between the self and the other, "the literal meaning of words can hardly provide anyone with what is conventionally called an ideal" (p. 7). By focusing on the problem of language, Aragon turns his narrative into an avant-garde adventure. He dissociates language from significance and discourages all naïve and foolhardy attempts to express the truth, the ideal. Aragon lays bare within the text the inevitable presence of error and confusion, stemming from the limitations of language as well as from accepted distinctions between right and wrong. By freeing the word from conventions he also sweeps aside all vestiges of romanticism, for if language is to be dissociated from the mimetic process, it cannot possibly represent movements of the heart. The inevitable separation between experience and expression has not placed Aragon in a quandary or reduced him to silence. It has on the contrary generated a verbal overflow or overkill, kindling the desire for and the voluptuousness of verbal indulgence. Even in the context of language we can find analogies with Fénelon, who had clearly pointed to the dissociation between feeling and expression; but the prelate's doubts and discoveries provide constructive criticism and plead for reforms. They do not lead to moral transgression or generate revolt even though he sees the threat of a breakdown. By foregrounding rhetoric, the seventeenth-century writer ultimately embellishes and codifies language, thus providing a model for future generations, whereas Aragon, far from limiting himself to any given type of language or discourse, multiplies and diversifies speeches, oracles, confessions, prayers, songs, invocations, negotiations, and exorcisms. In the most powerful passages words generate words whose dynamic interactions preclude all standards of measurement.

Yvette Gindine in her perceptive analysis of the novel suggests that Aragon's fiction is in a state of transition, for in *Anicet ou le panorama* his allegiance to dadaism had been far less critical.[4] In *The Adventures,* dadaism must indeed compete with other trends as well as with a peculiar textual corrosion repeatedly redirecting and disrupting the narrative. The final guffaws of God, which we can construe as the supreme disruption, the definitive dadaist act, take place in a typically surrealistic metaphorical setting.

We suggested in the beginning that *The Adventures of*

4. Yvette Gindine, *Aragon prosateur surréaliste* (Geneva: Droz, 1966).

Telemachus, Les Malheurs des immortels, and *Répétitions* teeter on the brink between dada and surrealism. *The Adventures* ends in destruction and derision, in the elimination of Telemachus and Mentor and in God's irrepressible mirth. The pursuit of dream and desire can be detected not only in the conclusion and in Mentor's irresistible "Smash everything!"; it is clearly articulated as early as Book III when he explains the Dd system. He undermines meaning, perverts feeling, perception, and knowledge by putting them on the same level. Mentor encourages his audience to perform, and "Smash everything!" functions as a battle cry.

The Adventures of Telemachus hardly ends as unpredictably as it would seem. Mentor begins his final lesson by referring to destruction and suicide, making the course of life indistinguishable from that of death. The nihilistic absurdity of dadaism happens to coincide in this instance with surrealist reliance on paradox, for indeed both approaches unleash the explosive power of language. Moreover, Aragon's metaphorization of love, his mockery of all conventions, his parody of a respected classic in no way derogate from what came to be regarded as orthodox surrealist practice. However, we do not emerge from *The Adventures of Telemachus* with a credo as we do from *Nadja*, or with the vision of a transfigured world as from *Le Paysan de Paris.* By dint of deviation, displacement, and derision, we delightfully descend into the diabolical nirvana of dada.

Translating a late dadaist work that displays surrealist traits poses, of course, difficult and sometimes insoluble problems. Few if any of Aragon's contemporaries could rival his dazzling verbal dexterity and his amazing virtuosity as a stylist in prose as well as poetry. Not only has he pushed ambiguity all the way to perverse equivocation for the legitimate dadaist purpose of perplexing and even vexing his readers, but in the third enclosed message arising from the depths he has gone so far as to seal off meaning completely and reach a state of perfect unreadability, capable of astonishing the most fervent deconstructionist. Our chief purpose throughout has been to convey an impression in keeping with that of the original work, however enigmatic some of Aragon's pages may appear and however ambiguous his ideas.

THE ADVENTURES OF TELEMACHUS

To Paul Eluard

A DUE APOLOGY

The problems of writing and of originality may for a moment torment a young writer; but they can in no way detain him. For some adventurous minds, 1920 proved to be the year of formal prosecutions. So far so good. The literal meaning of words can hardly provide anyone with what is conventionally called an ideal. It is a meaning that more often than not eludes me; and indeed the reader will recognize that throughout the book I have used the word "love" as a cover for a multiplicity of elements by no means essential to love itself. I shudder to confess that, for lack of words, even to this day I seek to explain by dint of remembered pleasures the true movements of my heart. Hence a number of errors, equivocations, confusions.

If the childishness of this work appears obvious to all, it is because these adventures, which do not go beyond the cycle of childhood, set an equation with two unknown quantities, man and woman, the solution of which must wait till later. Make no mistake: we venture to criticize life only in love's absence. As soon as the latter makes an entrance, the particulars of the problem change, and our acquiescence embraces everything. It is our indifference to ideas that we did not suspect. The satisfaction of testing ourselves at the mercy of an emotional hurricane. I break down in the grasp of infinite tenderness, accepted and finally revolting. Here begins the eclipse of the ego. Night at high noon. If you know what love is, make allowances for whatever follows.

L.A.

BOOK I

Despite the great wealth of our languages, the thinker often finds himself at a loss for the expression which exactly fits his concept, and for want of which he is unable to be really intelligible to others or even to himself. To coin new words is to advance a claim to legislation in language that seldom succeeds; and before we have recourse to this desperate expedient it is advisable to look about in a dead and learned language, to see whether the concept and its appropriate expression are not already there provided. Even if the old-time usage of a term should have become somewhat uncertain through the carelessness of those who introduced it, it is always better to hold fast to the meaning which distinctively belongs to it (even though it remains doubtful whether it was originally used in precisely this sense) than to defeat our purpose by making ourselves unintelligible.

KANT, *Critique of Pure Reason.*
2d Part, 2d Division, Book 1, Section 1
[Norman Kemp Smith Translation].

Like a seashell on the beach, Calypso disconsolately repeated the name of Ulysses to the foam that carries ships afar, unmindful in her sorrow of her immortal self. The seagulls in attendance took flight when she approached for fear of being consumed by the fire of her lamentations. The laughter of the meadows, the cries of the fine gravel, all the caresses of the landscape made her miss more cruelly the absent lover who had taught her to perceive them. What good did it do her to peer toward infinity, if she could see only the bitter plains of despair?

In vain did the island shores blossom upon the passage of their queen, attentive only to the ebb and flow of the tides.

Luckily, a boat broke to bits at the feet of Calypso. Two abstractions issued from it. The first, not yet twenty, looked so much like Ulysses that the shrubs, by the very way he folded them, recognized Telemachus, his son, who had yet to bend a woman in his arms. The second entity passed the comprehension of the sandy walks, of the desolate goddess, of eternal spring reigning in these fabulous lands; nobody, whether a nymph or even a loftier deity, could recognize Minerva under the aged features of Mentor.

Meanwhile, Calypso joyfully rediscovered her fugitive lover in that young castaway advancing toward her. Her foreknowledge of this body which she had never glimpsed before troubled her more than the shining spots of seaweed the surging waters had pasted on Telemachus's polished limbs. Feeling womanly, she gave a false display of anger and cried out: "Strangers, flee from here if you value your lives. Men are banished from my domains;" but her blushful countenance belied her speech. The young traveler bowed with the grace of a remembrance, saying, "Madam, you who appear so beautiful that I might well take you for a goddess, could you look without pity on a youth in quest of himself throughout the world, for indeed he pursues his own image: my father ceaselessly carried far away from me by the very same fury of tempests and concepts that thrusts me naked at your feet?"

— This father, who might he be?

— They call him Ulysses, and what good does it do him that his name is famous all over Greece and Asia? His fatherland is forbidden him; the waves won't spare him a single error; and his wisdom, far from steering him clear of reefs, always plunges him into new dangers. Without hope I left my mother, Penelope; I roam the Universe to bring her back Ulysses, engulfed perhaps in its depths, and, sometimes, I discover in men's minds the trace of the hero who eludes me and whose fortunes, if the bizarre play of passions ever tossed him on your isle, you would not, O Goddess, hide from his son, Telemachus.

Calypso, more attentive to the motions of her heart than to the movements of his speech, did not dare break, either by word or gesture, the charm that riveted her eyes to this all too human form. The dizziness that blurred her vision forced her, for fear of herself, to shatter all of a sudden the silence.

"Telemachus, your father . . . But I'll tell you his story in my dwelling where you will find a resting place softer and fresher than the curled wind of feathers ruffled by these attendants, and provided you know how to enjoy my motherly care, that happiness, that privilege of a moment, which, in the closed labyrinth of my immortal arms, I can endlessly prolong."

The Goddess's cave opened on the slope of a hill.

Its threshold dominated a sea more disconcerting than shifts of weather, multicolored among precipitous rocks streaming with foam, sonorous as sheet metal, and, on the backs of waves, the great wing slaps of nightjars. The inland regions brought many a surprise: a river descended from the skies and, in its passage, hooked on to trees blooming with birds. Villas and temples, unknown structures, metal scaffoldings, brick towers, cardboard palaces formed a heavy and twisted braid bordering lakes of honey, landlocked seas, triumphal ways; forests wedged into impossible towns while their hair vanished in the clouds; here and there the ground split open to the level of precious mines from which flashed forth the landscape light; the open air dislocated mountains and sheets of fire danced on the heights; pigeon-lamps sang in aviaries and, among the tombs, the buildings, the vineyards, strolled beasts stranger than a dream. The setting stretched to the horizon by means of maps and the deviant struts of a Louis-Philippe bedroom where angels slept, blond and chaste as the day.

When she had shown him all these natural beauties, Calypso told Telemachus, "Here you will find restful beds and clothing to suit you. After having made use of them, pray come to see me: I promise you tales to touch your heart."

At the same time, she led him together with Mentor into a retreat next to the cavern where she lived. Within, a marvelous climate prevailed, and objects radiated light;

clothing of snow, tunics subtle with sentiments, gowns of sensuality, cunning girdles awaited the new guests. As Telemachus dallied over the feel of the tissues, wondering at their incomparable lightness, Mentor rattled with laughter:

"Telemachus, will you ever find your father, if you allow yourself to be smitten by the delicacy of a fabric? One wool is no more beautiful than another, one wool is hardly more wooly than the next: errors lodge only in our judgments. Continuous inferences from experience to generalizations, sophisms more refined than these textures, such is life and its lies. Why complain about phenomena only to fall prey to pain or pleasure?

"Whatever," replied Telemachus with a sigh, "may urge a young man to rejoice or complain, your derision will curtail it. All the same, I have given some thought to dispensing with reliance on reflexes. But puppets have no control over themselves: either machinery or self mastery, I lose myself between these poles. As soon as we obey, do we obey ourselves? On order depends the refusal of submission. You proffer your hand; my fist tightens and withdraws; and that too pertains to politeness. The gesture I have mentioned reminds me of death: we live by courtesy. But how lovable is that lady, Mentor, and what kindness she shows us!

"If you love her, Ulysses will leave you in the lurch. Just think of that. I don't see any difference between an attachment and flight from oneself. We admire in proportion to our stupidity and cherish in relation to our ignorance. Narcotic words put newborn hearts to sleep. Watch out for the tales of desire,—our own or the other's, for we can hardly tell where lurks the greater danger."

Calypso received them in the midst of her nymphs who brought them an ideal feast: they served the reasoning of the Medes, the coral of the songs of India, the penetrating fragrance of Egyptian vocables, the comely wisdom of Athens. Whatever flesh they prepared struck the guests as exquisite as sorrow. Wine, more insinuating than air, more delicious than memory, did not seem to them as fresh as the fruit, similar to good fortunes. The nymphs then began to sing. They told of the fighting between the elements and the dead; of the struggle between man and words; of the ardor common to gods and beasts, that phlogiston of the world, love with purple lips. Finally they recounted the labors of those heroes who had besieged Troy, the city of appearances. The name of wise Ulysses died like a sob in the vehement delirium of lyres. Hearing it, Telemachus lost himself in meditations which gave his features a singular beauty. Calypso, noticing that he could no longer eat, made a sign to her nymphs who started to dance and thus brought back to mind the pleasing image of sensual delight. At the end of the meal, the goddess bowed to Telemachus and said to him:

"Know, O son of great Ulysses, that no mortal may with impunity enter this isle without my special favor. Even shipwreck, only too frequent in these parts, could not save you from my wrath, unless love . . . but, alas! your father before you found that out without any advantage to himself. It was up to him to live here in an immortal state; it took immoderate love of his country to tear him away from me, to drag him toward miserable Ithaca, to cast him on the waves that swallowed him. Cautioned by so sad an example, assured of never setting eyes on Ulysses or your native rock, forget your losses: accept, Telemachus, my bed, my kingdom, and godliness."

At these words, the young man blushed and stared so intently at the body of the goddess that he paid but little attention to the tale of Ulysses' adventures. For fear of seeming naïve, he used the grief in which the king's death had plunged him as a pretext to hide his confusion and elude the offer of so sudden a happiness. Trusting that music would quiet the human heart, Calypso asked Eucharis to sing a soothing song. The beautiful nymph tuned her lute, and her voice rose like a torch:

"Rock, my strength! Sorrows, torrents, fetters of the night, snares of death sweeping upon you! Stick out your tongue of fire, devour all, satyr, coal of the forests. Get up! on a dark cloud the heavens for setting foot on earth. Gloom, the winds carry you away. The storm bursts in tremulous bells, lightning says: *God damn!* The earth opens like a sore and shows its womb. My feet are wheels, my hands are wheels, your eyes are wheels. In the nutcracker of your arms love breaks with the clouds, men's teeth under my fist, dried out trees spouting harsh language, broad panels of rough silk torn like chimeras, mechanical smokes, perfumes of the swamps."

In order to know her visitor better and read the language of his heart, Calypso asked the young man by what turns of fortune he had run aground on her shores. He declined for a long while, but she exerted so much pressure that his resistance broke and he proceded to recount his misfortunes:

"Having left Ithaca without the knowledge of my mother's evil suitors, I endeavored to seek information concerning my father from the other princes who had returned from the siege of Troy. Not one of them could tell me whether he was still alive; they generally believed that he had gone to Sicily, driven by violent winds. And there I resolved to join him. Mentor, my companion, strongly objected to my plan. 'Fear the danger,' said he, 'of falling into the hands of man-eating cyclops or of Trojans whose fleet cruises in those parts. Let us return to Ithaca: you will deliver your mother from the suitors' impositions, and if the gods don't give you back Ulysses, rule: one man is worth another.' Although I was too headstrong to heed him, Mentor did not abandon me."

While Telemachus spoke, Mentor, exhausted by the trip, had ceased to hold himself in check: luminous rays were escaping from his brow. Calypso looked at him with a mixture of astonishment and distrust: noticing this, the old man immediately extinguished the luminosity of his pate and assumed an air of modesty.

"The weather," Telemachus continued, "favored us at first. But suddenly a pitch black tempest engulfed us in darkness, pierced at times by the fire of heaven. It is by this ephemeral light that we glimpsed the ships of Æneas, as redoubtable to us as reefs. The pilot's confusion would have prevented any kind of maneuver had not Mentor assumed command and taken the helm. As I bitterly blamed myself for this foolhardy escapade, as I swore to Mentor that I would obey him in the future, this true friend answered with a smile: 'Your show of respect for my experience, save it for chariot racers. I do not wish to pass on to you a farthing of contrivance for shekels of wisdom. All of experience is tantamount to a tiresome turn of mind whereby, out of preference, we choose to expect the worst. The mask of old age does not differ from any other: it is no more than the borrowing of a name, a bauble, a grotesque and laughable hoax. Our habit of bestowing honors on bald or hoary heads will some day astonish people and lose all sense in the obscurity of childish myths. But in that enlightened period they will doubtlessly kill all newborn babes with green eyes. The previous century, youth, progress, middle age, our ancestors, moderation, hope: so many incomprehensible words that shake like so many plum trees the majestic beards of augurs. Telemachus, show that you are the worthy son of Ulysses and pay no more than fleeting attention to events that I did not foresee any better than yourself.'

"Having uttered these words, he got rid of the Trojans through trickery, and we reached the coast of Sicily by the strength of our oars. We can escape from one illusion only by substituting another; if we fancy that all is lost, no sooner do we realize our mistake than we imagine that we are safe. The utter prostration of weakness gives way to the extreme exultation of naïveté. On the shores of Sicily dwelled other Trojans, led by old Acestis. Upon our landing, they took us for some kind of enemy; in their first fit of anger they burned our ship and slaughtered all our companions. 'Understand,' Mentor told me, 'that because nothing can save us, neither can anything make us perish.' Indeed, they spared both of us in order to bring us before the king for questioning about our intent. Our hands tied behind our backs, covered with dust from the road we were thrown at the feet of this monarch who sternly asked about our place of birth and the object of our voyage. Our lies produced no other effect than an order to send us into slavery where we would tend to the flocks of the royal household. Assured, by listening to Mentor, that nothing could cause us to perish, I attempted to verify his axiom, and, stopping the guards who already were dragging me away, I cried out, 'King Acestis, recognize in me the son of Ulysses who prefers death to slavery!' All those present burst out in curses. Somebody identified me; and I was condemned to perish together with Mentor on the tomb of Anchises. I bitterly reproached my companion in misfortune for the false wisdom he had taught me. 'Everything strikes you as divine,' he answered, 'and you hold nothing back in your enthusiasms, but if a man or an idea affords you a glimpse of the device that props it up, you sing a different tune and your excessive contempt matches your misplaced adulation; once again you go on raving. My utterances are talismans, neither fortunate nor unfortunate. One word is just as good as the next: all of them are ciphers. And by the way, have no fear: people don't die for so little.'

"They had brought us to Anchises' sepulcher: they had by now erected the altars, lit the sacred fire; already flashed forth the sacrificial blade. Under torrential rains a hateful mob watched us march to our doom. Acestis, on a makeshift throne, attended our dying moments. The soldiers in the procession talked about their mistresses and made fun of us. My soiled clothing did not fit me. I had eaten only a horribly tasteless stew. It was all over; they were crowning us with flowers. At that moment, Mentor made use of a trick, and the situation was turned around. Sunlight filled the sky, and the people, moved to compassion, vehemently cried out that we be spared. The women were in tears. Our keepers respectfully freed us from our bonds. The king let his scepter drop, came down to meet us, hugged us and called us his friends, his saviors. At this marvel, I reverted to my admiration for Mentor. He laughed boisterously in my face and, in a few chosen words that now elude me, mocked my feelings of deference toward mere success. Acestis brought us to his palace and loaded us with gifts. Then he gave us a ship that would depart for Greece before Æneas's fleet could land in Sicily. Fearing to expose them to the anger of the Greeks, he refused to let us have a Trojan pilot and oarsmen, but provided us instead with a Phœnician crew, which had orders to leave us in Ithaca and return the ship to the island Trojans. But the conversational flukes frolicking with human thoughts held further perils in store for us."

BOOK II

Around us, I immediately saw that the various sentimental objects were no longer in their place.

ANDRÉ BRETON AND PHILIPPE SOUPAULT, *The Magnetic Fields.*

Of all of Calypso's nymphs, the most disturbing was Eucharis, so like the milk flowers that Telemachus would sometimes see in his dreams. During the young prince's narrative, Eucharis never stopped rolling on her transparent hands a long black lock tumbling from her brow. A single evening did not suffice to exhaust the adventures of Penelope's son. (How beautiful that woman must have been, surrounded by her suitors atop Ithaca's rock!) For many an evening Telemachus charmed the goddess and her companions with the voice of the only man then living on their island. Foliage pierced with light, restfulness slowly crossed by feminine apparitions on silent feet, days divided between siestas, softened by arbors, and hunting as exciting as the storm, with the lightning of long white hounds, mental aberrations amid the forest, on peaceful lake shores or within glades, sudden glances of heaven at the heart of asphalt trees. One night, similar to all the others, but darker, Eucharis visited Telemachus while he slept. He did not know at first by what name to call her. Then he found a host of insults as sweet as his tender awakening in the dark. The discovery of a body, how insinuating a pleasure. The carnal contact side by side, from heel to armpit, brings shudders that shake up nature like the flights of nocturnal birds. The youth turned on the side so lightly stroked, felt the mouth and breast of the stranger, then with a sweep of his unengaged arm he seized the woman's arm farthest from him and examined it until he reached its limit. Hair tumbled against shoulders, like a wave under a ship. A pinhole sun was born under four eyelids, broadened, broadened, and set the world on fire: "I am Eucharis," she said.

She quickly got up and ran to the neighboring cave. Telemachus felt heavier than the mountain. Eucharis returned with an oil night-light gleaming like a philosopher's stone: it seemed as golden as desire, and her lover hastily recognized the power of her beauty. Nymphs instill in mortals an ever renewed passion. Eucharis was a nymph and Telemachus a mortal. Weariness had long since made skulls turn in the shade when Eucharis's head fell back on the bed like an empty walnut shell. Telemachus then absentmindedly petted the forehead of his first mistress and began to think.

"Everything that is not myself is incomprehensible. Whether I seek it on the shores of the Pacific or pick it up in lands where I really live, the shell applied to my ear will resound with the same voice that I'll mistake for that of the ocean and that will be no more than the rumor of my own self.

"All words, if suddenly I no longer take pleasure in holding them in my hand like pretty nacreous objects, all words will enable me to listen to the ocean and discover in their auditory mirror no more than my own image.

"Language, contrary to all appearances, consists merely of I; and any word I repeat casts off everything that is not me until it becomes an organic noise through which my life is displayed.

"There is only myself in the world, and if from time to time I am weak enough to believe in the existence of a woman, I need only to bend over her breast to hear the pounding of my heart and recognize myself. Feelings are no more than languages that facilitate the practice of certain functions.

"In my left waistcoat pocket I carry a most faithful likeness of myself: a burnished steel watch. It speaks, indicates time, and does not understand anything about it.

"Everything that is myself is incomprehensible."

Eucharis's first glance was a desire. "Leave me alone, said Telemachus. There now. I assure you that you owe your latest triumph merely to the strange lighting of this room. I did not expect your visit. So much the better, we won't mention it.

— Child, how I pity you, and how your insolence offends me! What I find attractive in you is hardly your stupid pride: your black hair and your touchiness. So take it easy on your bed. Few people know how to enjoy that immobility sweeter than slumber, when man and woman are reluctant to separate while feeling only aversion for one another.

— Please let me sleep by myself. I am not used to taking my rest in company.

— Really, don't you know anything about love?

— That's none of your business. You taught me everything, but be assured that I'll be ever so grateful if you let me sleep instead of completing this tiresome education."

While Telemachus turned toward the partition a body immediately taken over by Morpheus, the nymph, her hair in disarray, jumped out of bed and stretched merrily, head over heels, more fully awake than in the morning. On the threshold of the cavern she stopped, looked at her hands, looked at the sea, looked at the wind, looked at the cataracts, the gullies, the plateaus on the rock, the laziness of flowers. She stooped, stretched her arms, touched the sky, touched the stone-loving ivy, touched the eternal snows, touched Eucharis, the most beautiful of the nymphs, the nymph triumphant, the mistress of young Telemachus, that reed asleep in its litheness, Eucharis . . . With the limpid water spurting from the rock, Eucharis rid herself of the recollections of love. Then she combed her long hair, the sole remnant of night in the world, and she started to sing and to braid, grapes or chains, tresses heavy with kisses:

"Foaming death at the foot of cliffs, the maple at the heart of the magnetic mountain that slips the anchor of ships, the sun my pretty spouse of dawn, indolent afternoons, the plunging flights of kingfishers. I would give the whole of life for my hair, my hair that revives with its stormy lozenge my friend's innumerable senses.

"My friend is a tiny seal, a cute glutton, my lover. My friend has given me nothing, he has not told me that I'm beautiful. He petted me by chance and we slept together. Slept, slept, slept. His hands are handsome white gods.

"Marine disclosures, your smooth seaweed kisses dance. You slowly slide between my arms, broken pine, pride, ebony or ice bank. Lizard, what do you say of my teeth? What have you to say about our weather? Hardly anything prevents us from going on vacation.

"Lunacy around the neck, furred embraces, in the meadows woman and lost desires. Love day and night. Whatever climbs out of the forest takes the shape of spring. In the shade of Telemachus, snuggles the whole of nature. Sing, vine shoots, fires, drafts; the golden insects await your awakening."

Old Mentor was climbing the slope, rolling in his mouth a pebble to loosen his tongue, as everybody knows. He saw Eucharis, heard her song and Telemachus's name.

— My child, he said to the nymph, have you listened to me? You were joyfully chattering all by yourself about my pupil.

— Stranger, said Eucharis, you have a peculiar conception of your tutorial duties. Nonetheless I am smitten with your prince. He sleeps like a perfect beast. See what he did to me. And here, and here again.

— Far better that he should have his initiation with you than with your fading and ever so wanton Calypso who had counted on it.

— After my mistress, it is I who . . .

— Not so fast, beauteous nymph, comb your hair and don't shout."

Eucharis continued her song: "Vigorous tree, my thief, to you belong the beaches, the plains, the foibles. Knot around my porcelain fingers the ribbon of your hair. Arid ardor, with my two knees against your breasts, I rock. A pedestal top for music, that's love my darling."

Along the shore Mentor unflaggingly practiced his eloquence. He shouted all in one breath tongue twisting sentences. Attracted by his voice, gulls flew around the old man and penguins formed a circle to listen to him. Purely for practice, he addressed to them the following exhortation: "If deeply felt and meditated, the thought of destruction would in a single day change the universe into a monastery or a tomb. When will we blush at playing the game of life? The shorter the farce the better. It has all been going on too long, man, birds, the rest. You who sleep in cities, those vast hospitals with numbered huts, where cemeteries are the freshest gardens, you are no worse than rustics astride their manure piles, stagnant ideas, bulbs of stupidity or decay of intelligence.

"God's work is beautiful, a fit subject for ecstasy. No matter if some day we must die as long as we have seen it, with its delightful palm groves, its mountains, its valleys, melancholy, little boats, two and two are four, the marvelous balance that proves the existence of the Creator, the joys of childhood, of youth, of maturity, of old age, madness, wisdom, Paris, Capital of France, the touching examples of filial piety, or pure love, of the sweet abnegation of self! The happiness of the day is unalloyed happiness.

"Freedom through suicide or evasion, we always return to this point in the story. But what do we know about such means of transportation? I have read many excellent pages on the following: red eiderdowns, glasses of wine. You will never convince me that the owner was stupid enough to have left his key on the door: a revolver shot, you never get off so cheaply. Where do they get the idea that people condemned to life should kill themselves? Prisons would be empty.

"Thought, where are you leading me? said the old fool. — To the tip of your nose, answered the little simpleton." There are people on the earth, they're just like lice. When you have finished making children, tell me. Afterwards, you might as well go at it again. The innocence of the newborn; there's another curious invention: we are all newborn, innocent, I mean guilty. Common sense, logic, ladies and gentlemen, what a death trap! They steal you blind, as in the woods.

"As this brief speech is beginning to tire you as much as life bores me, let us find together an escape from this trap. Like the peddlar who shows you postcards, then adds discreetly: How about some photographs, Mister? After such decent preambles I whisper in your ear the offer of a system disallowed by the Government, a brand-new, hot off the fire beautiful system, with a badge on which is inscribed: *Don't close the door*, a system, finally, a system, a system:

"*A* system.

"The Dd SYSTEM: night, cataract, generative power of minutes and of thoughts, clockwork jolting of feelings, desert wastes on oolitic paving-blocks (human eggs and ostrich skulls), broken chain of reason, watch chain!

"The Dd System: game of the white mirror on the black mirror, game of the white mirror on the flat mirror, game of the flat mirror on the convex mirror, game of the convex mirror on the concave mirror, game.

"The Dd system proposes:

"To resolve all problems in less time than it takes to say it;

"To set all problems in less time than it takes to think them;

"To sift out time, to shuffle confusion, to bug poor humanity to death;

"To bore stiff, to light the night, to obscure the day, to roll your good old goggle-eyes;

"To win or lose at every throw in games of skill and chance: Aunt Sally, bowling, knives, roulette, hobby horses, rhetoric, politics, poems, religions, loves, auction bridge;

"To unhook the sun, to extinguish enthusiasms sporting tiny full blown bellies;

"To shatter your logics so essentially logical, to make circles in the water, squares in the air, neither square nor round, neither in the air nor in the water.

"The Dd system proposes: to do this, that, the opposite, neither this nor that, nor the opposite, to do nothing, to do everything, to make you shut up and to die a tiny bit.

"The Dd system has two letters, two faces, two backs, admits all contradictions, does not admit contradiction, is without gainsay contradiction itself, life, death, death, life, life, life, caution to patrons.

"People who suddenly see us in the light remain startled: You are speeding toward death; life cannot be that pleasant for you every day; how unhappy you must be, where will all that lead you? Society is no longer possible under such conditions, you want the end of the world: you don't mean it; it's a manner of speech; but then you are an anarchist? Oh! Mommy! Mommy! Mommy! The gentleman is an anarchist!

"You think you can hide by putting your hands in front of your eyes. You have hopes of making everything simple, everything happy thanks to a few cowardly acts.

"Honest folks, you cannot sell your soul to the devil just because you feel like it. How can you come to a show carrying in your heart so many muskrats, squirrels, and other frightful rodents; illnesses, bankruptcies, adulteries, treasons, head colds? You come here to seek oblivion, its eyes as empty as those of statues. I pour you the liquor deception, railing against you because boredom, impatience, indignation, contempt, laughter as phony as your suspenders, are all you have to say. I am not the only one who is ugly, stupid, dirty, pretentious, a cipher, a cipher; all of you and myself form a pretty pair. An odd couple! Don't shout at me that my mind has gone astray: when I contemplate all you black sheep, I stick very close to my subject.

"The Dd system makes you free: bust everything, you flat-faced ninnies. You will be the masters of everything you break. They made laws, ethics, æsthetics to instill in you the respect of frail objects. Whatever is frail is fair game for breakage. Try your strength just once; after that I dare you not to continue. Whatever you cannot break will break you, will be your master. Shatter sacrosanct ideas, anything that brings tears to the eyes, shatter, shatter, I bring you without charge that opium more potent than any drug: shatter. Thrust everywhere your dubious fingers. Doubt is the darkest, the deepest well ever presented to you: falling into it means an endless descent that will provide you for eternity with the charming sensation of going down in an elevator.

"Doubt of doubt: you can always turn your bloody nails against the most childish ideas. You will never manage to doubt anything or break anything whatsoever. You remain still, you imagine you are moving. Weakness or strength, everything is a ditty. The wind that dances on mountain snows laughs uproariously at your insignificant teapot explosions. On a certain scale, there are no longer some fools, there are only fools. There is no reason to look forever at the world through the narrow end of binoculars.

"The first D in my system was doubt, the second will be faith.

"I believe in me, in you, in self, in all the others.

"I believe in miracles, in chances, in occult sciences, in Science, in soap, in the generosity of the heart, in public spirit.

"I believe the blue sky, the green trees, the tricolor flag, the red flag, the earth as round as a ball, young youth, old, old age. I believe. I believe in doubt, I doubt my faith. I doubt that I believe in my doubt. What I believe is that I believe it.

"What has been, what will be cannot prevent whatever is from being. What I have said, what I shall say cannot prevent me from saying what I do say. A white and black Janus, the Dd system will be the school of sincerity. A former minister of the Republic, Commander of the Legion of Honor and member of several learned societies, who financed with his own money the propaganda of the DADA movement, told me one day: 'In my entire career I have met only one sincere man: the banker Rochette.' Sincerely, between ourselves, are you sincere?

"An aim more variable than the weathercock's wind where the hunter turns with his game is indifferently in the direction of the two poles, dawn or dusk, we no longer know which, and the sun in spite of it all, golden flower of windpipes, plucked canary, innermost cry, sincerity is the air's common tender. In vain do they wave before my eyes the flag which stands for public opinion: admiration, contempt, indifference, all of this leaves me supremely unconcerned. Alone, facing the vast world, that little universe of your imagining, I am staring you in the face, without requiring anything, without seeking within you even this particle of stupidity which shivers in your orbits, and I laugh like a wheat field."

The frightened penguins made their escape while directing toward Mentor long cries of reproach and angry looks. "Am I, thought Minerva, the helmeted child of Jove or that garrulous Greek who proudly wears male attributes?" As he or she asked this question, Calypso appeared in a morning dress, her hair blown by the wind,

with a fresh complexion; and Minerva no longer enter-
tained any doubts about being a man. "Goddess, said
Mentor, you are more beautiful than the sands. Upon my
word of honor.

— What shame, old man, your word?

— If you don't believe my words, come close to me,
goddess, and you will find that your charms have restored
life to a man who had felt for the last fifty years that he
had been cut off from the living.

— How unusual, said Calypso, I believe that your
hair has turned darker.

— Expect more sensational miracles. Notice how my
limbs have regained by your side their strength and
elasticity.

— You are squeezing me like a young man. Oh!
Mentor!

— Let's wander together, Madam, into the depths of
this thicket.

And all that remained on the seashore was the polished pebble fallen from Minerva's mouth together with
howling birds making love in full flight.

BOOK III

With all the nobility you can imagine,
Sturel was creating for himself
the state of mind of an adventurer.

MAURICE BARRÈS, *The Call to the Soldiers.*

$\mathbf{A}$rmed with his bow and arrows, Telemachus carried with him in the island's woods an incurable melancholy. Vainly did the amorous birds sigh under verdant arbors the divine name of Eucharis; vainly did the waves, vainly did the leaves, agitated one by one by soft fingered zephyrs, murmur; Eucharis . . . Peering into natural basins, the young hero followed the trembling image of a body whose full power he no longer needed to measure. He had brought down a few flying flames, shot some furry boundings, and these victims were hanging from his belt. All of a sudden, through the foliage, what novel object impinges on his sight? Within a bucolic retreat, Calypso lying on the grass with Mentor! Mentor nestling in her arms.

The goddess's hair floats in the breeze; her veil no longer hides her gypsum breast: a languid, voluptuous conflagration, Calypso shines like a new penny in the grass. She bends her head toward Mentor, who, prostrate in the midst of caresses, devours his beloved, wasting and burning away in the consummation. From her mouth springs a nimble, creeping red fire. The phoenix ceaselessly blazes forth from this desire akin to words, falls to dust, and from its ashes returns to life with renewed passion. The vast alternating shivers of the tides shake this human bush, looped as by two swan wings by Calypso's harmonious coves. Mentor's right foot propped against an aspen trunk makes it reel in the sun. Suddenly, the old man's vigorous body is incurvated toward the sky, the earth seems to be engulfed beneath him, and through this living porch Telemachus sees the fields of heaven obscured by flights of birds and pastures slowly inhabited by cows. Garlands of senses monstrously twisting though the landscape: what god will skip this rope at vinegar churning speeds? The firmament rebounds on skulls like a child's ball, blue and black by halves. Low tree branches caught up in the chase brush against the hard breasts of the earth, moan, boomerang, and, lifted once more by the returning monsoon, split along protracted, white, pearl perfect, sensitized feather edges. For a moment the disunited bodies calm down on the moss and come into contact with one another only by delicate touches. The lovers gain breathing space by exchanging tenderly awkward attentions. The lands of laughter are further off than ever. The breath that bathes foreheads comes from life's limits. Stop. Love is day hemmed in on all sides by shadow: Mentor and Calypso remain silent; and secure in his hiding place, Telemachus scrutinizes their repose.

"O my friend, said the goddess, will you remain faithful to me? will you continue to think of me?

— Prolonged aging, answered Mentor, affords man the spectacle of a thousand happenings: I have already lived two hundred years, and my third age has just begun. The heavy hand of time dulls my senses. I can no longer remember a number of events that I witnessed as a youth: nonetheless, my memory retains an even greater number.

— How coldly you speak! What are you looking for?

— A round pebble, not too big. Don't bother; I have what I need.

— I can scarcely believe my eyes: by what prodigy, Mentor, have you recovered that remarkable energy: no young man had ever accustomed me to such passionate outbursts, neither the divine Ulysses, nor Bacchus

Eucomes, my former guest and most polished of the gods. You must be hiding some secret from me. A drug.

— That power that you have come to expect from the first passerby, why should it astonish you on the part of an old man? Can time, that banal infusion, also deceive goddesses?

— Say what you will, there is something here that passes my comprehension.

— Hey! why bother to understand? The animal for whom the airs and daylight are the only nurture adopts the color of the things it touches. A lynx's urine changes into coral. The human backbone, once the spinal cord has rotted in the grave, gives birth to snakes that remember dorsal shudders, nocturnal love or cold sweat, and hiss at night around houses. Several farmers have assured me that the field insect we see weaving its white gossamer around a leaf casts off its shape in exchange for a flying death head. Soil generates frogs. Buried animals, as we know by experience, transform themselves into bees who, friends of flowers, enjoy the countryside and eagerly work on their treasure, their dearest hope. Not far from Pallenis there are men whose bodies get covered with feathers fallen from the heavens at the end of the year. Reason, like the child ravished by an eagle, wanders among life's clouds. Everything slides, quoit of smoke, nimble quicksilver. Torrential centuries escape from mountains of shadow. Jostled by the sand of hours, I no longer know whether 'soon' lies just around the corner or arrived here a moment ago; and *just now* designates what eludes me.[1] Game of chance. Am I a child or an old man? Hardly have I marveled at the sun but my eyes grow dim, and yet our bodies—may the flames at the stake devour them, may time consume them—cannot suffer any evil, believe you me. Time's spiders, we run along its threads and deny the void. The flies our ideas buzz louder than the wind.

— Mentor, you are so tiresome: pet me."

No sooner had the earth ceased to moan like so many bed springs than travestied Minerva continued her speech, akin to the horizon. — "O Caly, she said, the world is at our mercy, the world can do nothing against us. I do not utter these words without reason: if I become hard hearted, the moon can no longer shine atop the heavens, eggs petrify under the hen, wolf devours man, trees tumble with loud cries. And how do the winds react to my thoughts? They blow away the leaves, but do not change them into words. Language alone persists in the universe like an inheritance: I have pity for the most precious jewels. The salt of the earth also dies, but the names that fall like figs on the heads of children survive their bearers, momentary dust. We have already forgotten the future: the kings of Europe, wars named after the

1. *Tantôt* and *tout à l'heure* can designate, according to context, an event that took place in a recent past or that will occur in a proximate future. There are no suitable equivalents in English. [Translator's note.]

length of their duration, the discoveries of the human mind, the knack of measuring roads by means of the terrestrial meridian. But we have remembered the syllables: CHAUCHARD inscribed in gold letters on the wall of a Museum of tomorrow."

Calypso was tracing emblems in the sand. Mentor took his mistress's hand:

"Calypso, your eyes are black.

— My eyes?

— Yours.

— That, Mentor, is a figment of your imagination.

— Could it be, Calypso, that you have malicious designs?

— Me? What do I know about evil?

— You draw very poorly; that feathered heart looks suspiciously like a flight of fly specks. And that dove? It has no wings.

— My, I no longer thought about them.

— Then what do you think about?

— About destiny, about glances that drown in ink, about the dust on garden paths.

— You're doing yourself harm, child, by counting the bars of heaven. You are not of an age to play with light effects.

— How the day has vanished. It's already evening! It's almost too dark to see. I'll have them bring torches.

— Do you feel like reading?

— I'm afraid of the twilight. Am I not mad? In the

morning I eat forests on buttered bread. At noon, the orange is on the ceiling. In the evening, with the tip of my umbrella, I write on the gravel of public squares the letters of a name . . .

— Whose name?

— A name. I meant a word, the first that comes to mind. For instance . . .

— Don't fib.

— What do you take me for? For instance Care, Song, Greatness. Don't get up, I'll give you what you want.

— I don't want anything. Oh yes, that pebble. Thanks. Your hand is very beautiful for a flower. Come close, clear water. You won't object if I call you by this name?

— That makes me crushed ice. Don't squeeze my wrist. You don't know your strength.

— Why, my little sea otter, do you let your veils slip down to the ground?

— Me, me? Out of habit, out of negligence, out of fear of ridicule.

— Why do you tremble?

— Because you stare at me, because my hair is in a mess; because a green tree in the forest, on which I have often imprinted different initials, is waiting for me.

— Your mouth is full of stars, laugh a little.

— I don't dare.

— Your lips are summers.

— Ah! it's as beautiful as on the stage.

"Not again," exclaimed Telemachus in his brake. "Let's leave these Kangaroos alone and go to bed."

On the threshold of the cave, Telemachus inopportunely found Eucharis laying in wait for him. He wished her a good evening, kissed her on the forehead and tried to dismiss her. But she strenuously objected and made him understand that honor required that he appear fit and display his conquest: "Do you imagine, she added, that I take a lover just for his good looks? A nymph needs a man so she can speak before him, walk in the meadows without fear of satyrs. Hunting all day, coming back late, going to bed with your boots on, bullying ever so slightly a sensitive servant when you wake up, that would be your way of life, you chauvinist louts, if we did not set things right. Telemachus, this very hour you must attend a play. An amateur company of water sprites is putting on a show tonight, and the whole island is converging on a place called False Rocks. Look, I am wearing my electric bow, my storms, my heaviest look. Don't they bring out my beauty, and aren't you just burning to display yourself in my company? Hurry up and get dressed. Look, here's a moon pin: pour on your hair the powder of golden carabids."

The locality named False Rocks was an amphitheater of clouds in the countryside. The tiers were collapsing under a crowd of divinities made for scaling the heavens. The action, which had started long before Eucharis's and

Telemachus's arrival, unfolded on a central set consisting of luminous water. A group of water sprites representing a chorus of youths enamored with truth sang in measured tones precepts of wisdom. Other performers dressed like old men made fun of them and interrupted their recitation by blowing into little iron trumpets. The young men spoke of life; they were the prey of scruples more beautiful than daylight, and at the very moment when they felt sincere, they still imagined they were lying. "I lie if I say I lie," they perpetually lost their way in the depths of this labyrinth: Epimenides' syllogism. The old men laughed, stuck out their tongues and asked them if by any chance they had slept fifty-seven years in a cave. At the same time, the old men childishly worshiped stones, pieces of cardboard, the resonant wind that some of them drew from large wooden mechanisms, the words of the puniest among them. In their turn, the young men shook with their laughter the cacti surmounting their heads, and their gibes enraged the ridiculous cultists. A burlesque battle ensued. "Is this supposed to be funny?" Telemachus asked Eucharis, but like the other nymphs she was clapping her hands and throwing bracelets and rings to the actors. In the great loge toward which the leaders of the chorus had turned, Mentor and Calypso were conversing with Neptune, the goddess's guest, smoking a meerschaum pipe and, from time to time, tossing trees of coral on the stage. Telemachus was doing his best to follow the play when one of the young water sprites bowed to Calypso and said:

"However slowly I open them, my eyes can sustain only one light, even sweeter to them than your anger is to my heart: the light of friendship where doubts dissipate like impotent little bee hives, a friendship which leads me to the end of the earth where I remain lost and ever waiting.

"You find me today in a state of abominable sadness. Whatever darts from my heart turns into a fireless rocket. That image will displease you. You are already bored. I won't even go on insulting you. Who knows where weariness begins or where it may end? You are looking at me and I am looking at you. What innocuous infamy by way of a holy palm will you aim at me next? I do not seek to reduce you to silence or force you to shout. At present, I feel no more than a great emptiness within me because of all those who befriend me in the same way as all the drops in a river befriend the drop of water they carry off to the sea. If you wish to answer for someone, you assert: I am as sure of him as of myself. Now, the one person in the world about whom I can have no psychological assurance is myself. The law of my being eludes me; or what continuous change enables others to recognize me and call me by my name; nor can I see myself in profile. At every moment, I betray myself, I fail to keep my own word, I contradict myself. I am not the person in whom I would place my confidence. Why despair for so little? Well you know that it takes no more than a glance from my friends to reduce my projects to chaos: we are friends for no other reason. I give up everything just to waste my time with them; I abandon myself. You think no doubt that I place in them the trust that I refuse to myself? Don't you believe it! I know their faults, and too many of their actions offend me. They do things that I would refuse to do at any price.

"I realize that they have precious little affection for me. We have not for quite a while brought with us those tiny scales by which we judge individual merit. I do not believe in my friends just as I do not believe in myself.

"My friends are those very people at whose mercy I have put myself for stupid but strongly emotional reasons. A torrent drags me along; I recognize it as my master and coax it with my voice.

"You who remain transfixed in this hall like a mud puddle, do not ask me by what road I'll take leave of this world, nor what bends me to an alien force. The man whose body is henceforth caught in a trap speaks to you serenely: do not listen to the words he formulates, hear only the monotonous song of his lips.

"You find me today in a state of abominable sadness."

. . . .

— What is the title of this play? Telemachus queried with a yawn.

Eucharis replied: "The Adventures of Telemachus, my darling."

BOOK IV

For me, Friday or Sunday is Monday.

FRANCIS PICABIA, *Purr Verse.*

Neptune had brought to Ogygia magnificent presents for beautiful Calypso. The night after the performance at False Rocks, while Neptune himself, Mentor, Telemachus and their hostess lay with the most familiar of the nymphs on restful couches voluptuously adorned with kisses, nimble fish spread before the guests those marvelous gifts, fresh from the abyss. In vessels of liquid lava slumbered the waters of submarine lakes enclosed in caverns, their rocks covered with resonant forests. Flying dolphins displayed their skins, changeable as the sands of the deep or the sprightly glances of Arethusa, that smiling fountain amidst the seas. The green fabric of currents, the phosphorescent tapestries of the depths were cast on the pink granite of the aerial cave. These unconscious treasures of the Oceans, these succulent fruits of concealment consisted of bygone thoughts, days of failure fallen one by one in the water since the Chaos, the lost desires of engulfed centuries. There were also tissues of shadow, crime's delights, the interferences among all earthly vices, paroxysms of nights. Telemachus received for his share three bottles brought by the waves of time, cast later by hands in distress into the upstream flow of ages, stranded on distant madrepores and triply chanced upon by a triton, that love had led astray to the ends of the world. On those glass bottles, which might contain life's main secrets, appeared in bold relief the block letters of three words:

OLD TOM

GIN

Calypso, Eucharis, and all the other nymphs implored the young prince to open immediately those transparent mysteries. Despite Mentor's advice, Telemachus, who no longer felt the same respect for his master since he had surprised him with Calypso, Telemachus, susceptible to the goddess's teasings and convinced that Mentor out of jealousy wished to prevent him from pleasing his mistress, Telemachus tried in vain to uncork the first bottle. Neptune in turn exerted himself to no avail. All the deities present made impatient use of their palms in their attempts to remove the cork of centuries anchored upside down in the neck. Already Calypso had signed and dated a note to Vulcan; already the zephyr ordered to carry it to the ironworks of Sicily was preening his wings with mountain water, when, to everybody's uproarious amusement, Mentor asked for the bottle; Eucharis was convulsed with laughter that a usually wise and restrained old man should have such pretentions. Neptune was guffawing in his beard, and streams of joy flowed from his eyes. Mentor took the bottle, brandished it, and smashed it against a rock.

From the fragments issued a sheet of paper, which Telemachus seized in his hurry to read it; but he felt mortified at his utter failure to decode the contorted lettering of the document. Mentor removed the leaflet from Telemachus's hands and read without difficulty:

ELSEWHERE, ONE DAY OR ANOTHER

"Lost on the shores of a bottomless lake where an unknown sky catches its own reflection, will I ever succeed in joining to my existence the human centuries whose obliterated trail, it would seem, cannot possibly cross these regions. I have forgotten even the direction of time, and I have no way of deciding whether I am moving toward yesterday or tomorrow. It is impossible here to know if the ages have come to a final stop or whether they precipitate their flight at the uniformly accelerated velocity of a stone nearing the ground. If only I had a chronometer to extricate myself from these uncertainties! A diffused brightness perpetually prevails in this world; and the sun of space, which is also that of time, has deserted this immutable firmament. The beautiful sheet of water closing my horizon swells toward the west and receives on the northwest a stream heading from the north. As I have somehow ascertained with the help of a compass, its direction appears to be north-northwest and south-southwest. But how can I measure its size? I have circled the lake several times without managing to assess, within a year or a minute, the length of the trip. Nonetheless, I had at first judged the circumference to measure one hundred kilometers. Further conjectures enabled me to increase this number to one hundred and fifty or one hundred and sixty kilometers. Its true measure must lie somewhere in between. The time I take to complete the trip cannot provide me with a guide line: it varies from a few thoughts to a desert of boredom and impatience. The beatings of my pulse do not inform me any better; their irregularity may result from my incapacity to appreciate any kind of equality in the midst of this appalling nature. Vegetable species follow in their development neither the usual plan nor the habitual order of succession: flowers become roots, trees grow toward the ground. Suddenly I imagine that I grow older while raising my eyelids. No mistake, I function rather poorly as an hourglass.

"I still wonder how I could have lost myself in time. I had accepted with pleasure an invitation to go to Normandy where one of my friends, the recently married Céleste P. . . . , has a villa. With Paris practically deserted, the prospect of spending a few days at the seashore in the bracing atmosphere of brine and fresh air delighted me. But I did not suspect the parlous states awaiting me in this land of peace and tranquillity. The day had been splendid. Dust had invaded the compartment, but as soon as we approached the sea a delicious coolness established its reign in our hearts. Upon arrival, I looked around and saw that the sky was sky blue. Céleste came toward me, his hand extended, when low and behold, my mind wandered, and I thought of something else. Once you have thought of something else, it's all over. In no way could I return to my point of departure and, from one thing to the next, I found myself in a desert region at an undetermined period of the universe. At first I did not understand what was happening to me. I said to myself: "It won't last." Now I no longer know if it is still lasting.

"I have ascertained that in the temporal blind alley where I have lost my way there is not a living soul. Only a companion in misfortune could enable me to come back to life. Together we would reconstitute time. Purely a question of comparison. But alone, I elude myself by dint of believing that I remain identical: if I stay the same from one minute to the next, how can I experience the quality acquired at this movement of the hand? Finally I no longer feel the continuity of my thought; strictly speaking, at certain moments. For the most part, everything seems logical to me in my solitude, and if I write for problematical rescuers, eyeless savages or the irresponsive waves that will carry off my bottle, I can no longer rest assured that the language I use will ever be intelligible to anyone but myself. I find rereading impossible: I understand myself only within the moment. The words that come to mind wear at times odd faces, bare and perhaps different from themselves. Pricked balloons. Pastimes, pleasures, leisures strike me as strange customs: fire is what I consider the most mysterious. The novel I had brought along for the trip had remained in my pocket; in its pages I find my only recollections of human life—a paradoxical life, hemmed in by the most elementary questions. I'll take an example from my book: a character named George, an innkeeper. Shop signs swing sadly in the blue city of sight. That self-limitation, the branch of holly that a man hooks one morning on his door condemns him for ever to be nothing but the innkeeper. In books, sudden lights begin to shine among the conventional characters we would like to be. The choice between two destinies vanishes tragically in the ragged movements of the heart. A gorgeous woman, two or three singular exaltations, an instant of perfect bliss, the entire existence of a citizen of the world come down to a few metaphors, more dismal and common than a carpenter's workshop. By dint of staring into emptiness, we feel, twisting in our breasts, the image of a blue and red infinity where life moves along at its usual pace. Adjusting in order to observe the universe or to question one's heart, neither one of these operations can proceed without weariness. It all ends with a lantern swinging in the breeze and, later, their load delivered, horses elated that they may at last trot along suburban highways.

"Ground of unrelated cries, of rank weeds, the earth runs who knows where; and with approving little grins we hold tightly against our vest pockets the tables of physical law. How artlessly we wrap together with our ribbon formulas a nosegay of daisies and roses, the functions of space and time, too indulgent to object! In the meantime, I feel more and more—I was going to say day after day—that the elements of knowledge, in their growing confusion, amalgamate. If I let two or three ideas get away, I'd destroy my last chance of returning to the land of clocks. What frightens me is a slow dissolution of my personality. Because of my loneliness, I cannot go mad. The sponges of silence, the crystals of emptiness, where was I? I hurry, a cyclist at a loss after the departure of his rear wheel and miraculously balancing himself on a single renewed revolution. Fear steals along, making its stormy little day. I suffocate more or less in accordance with the phases of my breathing because of my inability to distinguish them. You wouldn't believe what has become of sensuality in this whorish mess. The geometrical progression of desire becomes inconceivable where succession no longer operates. The four operations, wouldn't you know it! Vinegar fly, inkwell of the clouds, who will give me back the waffle decorated in relief with an Eiffel tour, the City of Lights, as they call it?"

— Just a minute, exclaimed Calypso. I expected that we would be talking about love. Oh! well, I sure was wrong.

Mentor was already smashing the second bottle. It appeared empty. He had to shake it in order to remove a rolled and rumpled sheet which he proceeded to read out loud:

ATTEMPTS TO ENTER INTO CONTACT
WITH MARS

New York, May 16.—Dr. Frederick Millener was able to convince himself that the planet Mars, during the three days of its greatest proximity to the earth, did not send us any message by radiotelegraphy. He had installed for the occasion in Omaha, Nebraska, a remarkably clever device. The receiving antenna consisted of thirty-five thousand miles of wire attached to masts and covering about twenty-five square miles. After vainly listening for seven days, he was in a position to declare that Mars was making no attempt to enter into communication with Earth. Following his experiment, the professor made the following announcements:

"We are not discouraged by the negative results of the

experiment. We did not undertake it in order to prove that radiotelegraphic signals were sent, but merely to discover whether such signals were being emitted. We would have been happy to announce to the world the reception of signals coming from another planet. Furthermore, we realize that there is no reason why interplanetary communications should not be established at some later date provided intelligent beings exist on the other planets.

"During the first night, we began to listen at 8 P.M. We initially tried 15,000 and 18,000 meter wavelengths. For several hours, it seemed that we could hear everything that was happening in the entire world. We heard Berlin, Mexico City, and all the important stations. A violent storm broke out somewhere; the sound of thunder was comparable to the noise produced by a violent hail storm on a zinc roof. At about 2 A.M., all was quiet again. We increased the wave lengths: this brought us to regions extremely distant from Earth. At that moment reigned a deathly silence. For several hours we gradually increased the wavelengths, until we finally reached 300,000 meters, but still without the least result. Now, if the other planets are inhabited, if science, on these planets, has progressed as much as our own, their inhabitants must possess an exact knowledge of terrestrial movements."

— This time, said Telemachus, I cannot understand a thing. The Sibyl is clearer, Delphos more explicit: I have rarely felt so utterly benighted.

The third bottle was uncorked without difficulty; and no sooner had Mentor taken from it a manuscript covered with purple characters, than a nymph filched it for prominent display on her living room mantlepiece. Mentor read the following:

"Hello, little one, country church after the plains of absence this way. In the midst of furrows without order the horizon turns. They, at the same place by which by which. The eyes of the stranger are playing cards. We seek this loss forever, face tanned by but in order to of one. Failed adventure. The glances of the passed bicycles leave a striped trail in our heart. A man or a woman carries off why as one was born just before we quickly carry her to him in the woods. The blackthorns of the slope shouts will stop with O sour nudes while you take advantage fails to keep an appointment with us gasoline engine. One across warns me and I turn around when the great threshing machine, Madam in conversation. She at the bannister of a cloud staircase tiny steps smiling at the catalogues of department stores and because will coil shoulders snake desired him. Question of happiness if hair from top to bottom in the noise they made love to unfrocked nettles, peace. It's how, aneroid barometer. Beyond my they possessed I for instance love enough. Resolution resolutions melts becoming to. Escaped, the so very beautiful, very pure, touchstone of everything let us estimate. At the mercy of caresses one day or another appeared because. To snicker you require considerable emotion. Now, akin to stars, yesterday as henceforth, morrow without precedent. I say the thing as my you and we stone in the void future with hands of he bloomed. With the shutters of therefore coal tree memories lived will become motionless we were along the river what is the date and in front of the red plush armchairs. Wheel write the goal later, waved handkerchief I wait: navigators begone.

"From when to voluptuousness the Is childhood jumped with will regret you dust of it or it of premium." Thus do reasonable people exhort me to resist. Joke to appear known that celestial avid scenery my let go by habit they will break. Silence of novel, the clocks with docile covering of the nevertheless you judged: have a nice day and.

"My life follows somebody's wake.

"MARCEL."[2]

Lake of the 4 Cantons, the 18th day of the month.

Calypso's island teetered on its moorings.

2. No doubt the famous Marcel Duchamp, a fellow dadaist. [Translator's note.]

BOOK V

Pussy, petsy, pussy cat, my kitty cat,
my wolfsy, my tiny ape, lovely snake,
my little melancholy monkey.

CHARLES BAUDELAIRE, *Intimate Journals.*

"Finally, said Eucharis, what do you want with your father?

— Knowledge of the past, that dorsal night, marks the beginning of all knowledge. At least, that's what they say. The child learns how to walk in leading strings. Later moves in all directions. I float on my back in time: that's how I call looking for Ulysses in my peculiar language. Once I have mastered mechanical secrets, I can go anywhere. Half turn to the right in the centuries. After that, I'll practice on the double. There may be a way to extend indefinitely life's regions; if we knew how, we would never die." Telemachus snuggled his stormy head between Eucharis's breasts, and his voice died down, a sea wave, against those golden heights.

"Eucharis, he said.

— Telemachus?

— Eucharis,

Eucharis, Eucharis, Eucharis, Eucharis, Eucharis, Eu-
charis, Eucharis, Eucharis, Eucharis, Eucharis, Eucha-
ris, Eucharis, Eucharis, Eucharis, Eucharis, Eucharis,
Eucharis, Eucharis, Eucharis, Eucharis, Eucharis, Eu-
charis, Eucharis, Eucharis, Eucharis, Eucharis, Eucha-
ris, Eucharis, Eucharis, Eucharis, Eucharis, Eucharis,
Eucharis, Eucharis, Eucharis, Eucharis, Eucharis, Eu-
charis, Eucharis, Eucharis, Eucharis, Eucharis, Eucha-
ris, Eucharis, Eucharis, Eucharis, Eucharis, Eucharis,
Eucharis, Eucharis, Eucharis, Eucharis, Eucharis, Eu-
charis, Eucharis, Eucharis, Eucharis, Eucharis, Eucha-
ris, Eucharis, Eucharis, Eucharis, Eucharis, Eucharis,
Eucharis, Eucharis, Eucharis, Eucharis, Eucharis, Eu-
charis, Eucharis, Eucharis, Eucharis, Eucharis, Eucha-
ris, Eucharis, Eucharis, Eucharis, Eucharis, Eucharis,
Eucharis, Eucharis, Eucharis, Eucharis, Eucharis, Eu-
charis, Eucharis, Eucharis, Eucharis, Eucharis, Eucha-
ris, Eucharis, Eucharis, Eucharis, Eucharis, Eucharis,
Eucharis, Eucharis, Eucharis, Eucharis, Eucharis, Eu-
charis, Eucharis, Eucharis, Eucharis, Eucharis, Eucha-
ris, Eucharis, Eucharis, Eucharis, Eucharis, Eucharis,
Eucharis, Eucharis, Eucharis, Eucharis, Eucharis, Eu-
charis, Eucharis, Eucharis, Eucharis, Eucharis, Eucha-
ris, Eucharis, Eucharis, Eucharis, Eucharis, Eucharis,
Eucharis, Eucharis, Eucharis, Eucharis, Eucharis, Eu-
charis, Eucharis, Eucharis, Eucharis, Eucharis, Eucha-
ris, Eucharis, Eucharis, Eucharis, Eucharis, Eucharis,
Eucharis, Eucharis, Eucharis, Eucharis, Eucharis, Eu-

charis, Eucharis.

> Clouded panes what an embarrassment
> With light of day at a closed casement.
> My heart almost lacks the daring
> To undertake your unveiling.[3]

Eucharis, Eucha-

3. Ogygian saw. [Aragon's note.]

ris, Eucharis.

BOOK VI

Repel incredulity. That will please me.

ISIDORE DUCASSE, *Poems.*

"Have you so far forgotten my lessons, Mentor asked Telemachus, that you should mourn those imaginary demises that Calypso so cleverly announces in the hope of keeping you on her isle? The other day, it was Ulysses; this morning, Penelope. Death, a mere linguistic contrivance, exists only in time, an unreliable method to account for events which someday will be discarded by mankind in favor of a more suitable system of expression. You can be assured that eternity will then become an immediate notion. The glaring weakness of a temporal conception appears in the very language that imposes its reality: the relationship between time and language has no more than an apparent necessity, the vocabulary of space makes up for it, and we make use of a term with a dual purpose in mind. Although the idea of time seems in itself obscure, the mind grasps it by indirection in conjunction with events, so indistinguishable from duration that in popular speech the latter lends them its name. Hence two inverted operations in naming harvesttime "l'août"[4] and in referring to years as leaves. Seeing an exiguous time span as the twinkling of an eye, a flash, etc., requires quite an effort of the imagination. But to call a mantle an evening wrap for reasons of coincidence does no more than extend the meaning of a term. The first operation, by no means easy, has only metaphorical in addition to conventional value. I consider the second one more satisfactory: what struck me as unintelligible: *one hundred years*, for instance, designates my contemporaries of the words *the century*, and by simple substitution provides me with a clear and defined term.

— You appear to trust space more readily than time.

— Right you are; I show some tenderness toward space, but that is because it furthers my delight, which time on the contrary curtails. Will you please leave me in peace or else read beforehand the *Flyer on the Preposition*

4. *Août*, meaning August, refers metonymically to harvest. [Translator's note.]

After: learn how to expound for an hour metalleptic cata-chresis, and then perhaps you will weigh your words before opening your mouth.

— On the day I give up this lightheaded talk, in spite of your belief in immortality, in spite of your old age which is haler than the butterfly nets of Spring, you will be dead, Mentor, utterly dead.

— You appear to delight in the prospect.

— I am indeed beginning to detest you as I do other old codgers. You deny time which gives me an advantage over you, your white pate turns down life under the pretense of refusing death, but I, Telemachus, I am all litheness and strength, unwearied by my effort I can re-peat it from the beginning, I can stand my ground, I won't let anybody put one over me and I'll go on sneer-ing. You know, when you are dead, I'll speak of you with bated breath and I'll use your authority in arguments in order to validate axioms favorable to my thesis. I despise you because of your imbecility, and you will belong to me in the future in the same way that the past belongs to the present which turns it to good use, makes light of it, and ruins it.

— Enough, we will soon be in agreement. You have made astonishing progress.

— That's truer than you think. The mantle of self-sacrifice sooner or later gets lifted by a breeze; and so we discover, if Mentor does his utmost to demonstrate Calypso's treachery, what jealous attachment rivets him to that beauty who is only too eager to indulge in more decorous passions.

— The son of Ulysses will always distinguish himself from other men by his moderate speech.

— You old hypocrite; while you slept, I saw on your chest those tatoo marks, that dermal complex bearing witness through the years, that cynical companion of perversity. At the very moment I unmask you, I can still see on your face that dignified air from which you never depart.

— I am curious to see to what extremes those momentous discoveries will lead you.

— Let me satisfy that curiosity: I am going to see Calypso and invite her to bed.

— Go.

— We'll laugh at your expense.

Telemachus went off, convinced that Mentor would stop him in his tracks. After a few steps, he was amazed not to hear his name uttered in an imploring tone of voice. He stopped, turned around and said:

— I'm going to sleep with Calypso.

Mentor appeared to show polite interest in the news. Telemachus, abashed, repeated: "I'm going to sleep with Calypso unless you give me a good reason not to.

— I? But are there more reasons for sleeping alone than in company? Sleep, sleep, bless you, it will serve you right.

— What? You won't stop me?

— Do you feel like going to bed with Calypso?

— Indeed not.

— So leave her to her nymphs.

— Ah! that's more like it; I'll rush off to her bed."

Mentor shrugged his shoulders and started to play ball with a pebble. Meanwhile, Telemachus expectantly thought about the goddess and tried to discover in her image the justification of some future rapture. In running through the mountains toward Calypso's cave, he almost knocked down Eucharis and passed by her without seeing her. She looked at him, understood everything, and went into hysterics. Already the prey of his own imagination, Telemachus hurried on too slowly to keep pace with his desire. But he found the goddess in full fledged conversation with Neptune. She told him: "Sit down, my friend," and gave him no more attention. After that she received her milliner and made plans about new hats. Finally she dismissed him with a smile. Livid with rage, he rushed about the fields, breaking the heads of all the decoys he encountered. He thought of Mentor and swore like a drunken sailor. In the neck of a wood he found Eucharis in tears, called her stupid, and as she redoubled her sobs, gave her a thorough thrashing. Exhausted by this effort, he gratified the desire that Calypso had awakened; nor was Eucharis finicky about the quality of the sentiments he showed her. She indeed proved so undemanding in this respect that Telemachus, having left her and chancing upon Calypso at the edge of a brook, felt sheepish when this lady greeted him with all manner of sighs and embarrassing simpers. Calypso burst into laughter, excused herself, and invented explanations for so surprising a collapse. But she lost control of herself and rushed off like a madwoman, forgetting her veils together with less chaste accessories. At this very moment, Telemachus's strength returned. He very nearly called back the fleeing goddess, but fear of ridicule prevented him. He got up, bathed in the sea and swam to a little reef, rather far from the shore, on which he climbed; he sat down, tore off some mussels which he ate raw while thinking of death. At this precise moment, Neptune was leaving Ogygia to regain his billowy palace. He hailed Telemachus in passing; and as the young man did not budge from his rock, he tacked in his direction, shouting: "Do you want to sleep with shark-women? sawfish-women? tortoise-women? phosphorescent women? electric mermaids? Do you want to know the bottom line of everything? the fate of sailors who excited the desires of waves? Do you want to enjoy pleasures about which the gods speak only in whispers? Do you wish to see the beast with a deathly name, the sea serpent that will destroy the world? Would you like to see the obscene little maneuver of quick sands? seaweed loves? submarine putrefactions? Enter, enter, pay when you leave!" Telemachus saw once more the impudent face of amorous Eucharis, the impertinent laughter of Calypso, the shrugs of Mentor, and deciding not to set eyes on the isle for quite a time, he rode behind the god of the seas. The trip must have been long, for the son of Ulysses had grown a beard by the time he reached Neptune's dwelling. He could have sworn, however, that their navigation had lasted no longer than the interval of two tides. He was received by seemly old divinities who, casting down their eyes, led him to a hall of rock salt where the most dazzling nudities seemed to await his arrival. They proceeded to dance around him: they were sponges, pearls, corals, lichens, shells, currents, sea horses akin to sinuous kisses. They perfumed the traveler, stripped him of some scruples, combed him and caressed him to death. Then the festivities began: everything that roams the world of imagination, the deserted world of unutilized spaces, the unconscious world of horned, feathered and gilled beasts, the vast world of glances with the rank germinations of poplars covered by snowy blasts, with the mortal embraces of great spiders, dashed, spout of instincts, shock, conflagration, love, into the showroom where a reborn Telemachus was gaining knowledge of perpetual delight. The Mongolian goat dormant in all of us awoke. Sturgeons coursed in the veins. From nocturnes of tresses arose stags and birds: childish hunting, obscure faces, tender tempests of glances thronged. The fauna of storms roused by the dogs of heaven with flashing teeth, a gala of immoderate and lost senses, opened restless eyes behind time's foliages. Earwigs danced! Loons initiated an endless night; majestic male goats passed on the horizon;

amid tranquillity's drowned hands, ermines glided along moss carpets; goldfish moaned more softly than happy women. Then came Boreas's monstrous nymphs, the beautiful shiny hindquarters, the oily and firm flesh of northern seas; I look at them, and the slow, powerful, listless to and fro movements of these pillars of life carry away, like a lopped-off ear, sharp-throated desire, the offspring of their passage. I know myself only as rapture, reptilian motion: blood, blood, blood. My hands, leaden spoons, twist and melt. My body is a circled barrel whose bursts will be more beautiful than thunder; it lifts with the dregs and the hoarseness of my voice. My knees elude immobility like those of machines. Prodigy's missile, dagger I depart and kiss I return. The world put to sack succumbs, a cistern under heaven's cataracts, bursting with my weight hurled down without choice on a random prey: discovery of a toothsome continent, I met the woman, my disease. Exclusive domain of touch, this body unnoticed by eyes preoccupied only with the hair that sprouts in making love, this body spreads out and stiffens against my flesh, deliberate contact. Awkward help steers passion toward delight, makes the couple sway, whale on the back of liquid plains, exchanging embarrassed and naked words, null and come from afar, followed by the streaming noises of clenched teeth, bitten off pieces, sudden vulgarities, precious, piercing. The right word, opened sluice gate, reveals the male's attention, the precise worry, the vital point. A couple out of legends, the merry-go-round goes round, grating, sharp, shrill, shrieking. My fist if you shriek once more. How it lasts, little gooseberry, my rocker, how it lasts. Your arm flees, unfastens. I no longer know, porcelain, don't ask me anything. I would like to sleep without displacing myself from your forest.

Meanwhile, Telemachus floated to the surface like an air bubble and swam to the island where Calypso awaited him. He found the goddess in a terrible state, blaming herself for Telemachus's departure and bitterly reproaching herself for having laughed at him. Eucharis, during the long absence of the son of Ulysses, had given birth to a child named Misochronopoulos, or more familiarly Miso, on whose face Calypso sadly recognized his father's features. Mentor, unable to stand children and considering Calypso a nuisance, had taken advantage of all this time to build by himself a ship and its rigging. Telemachus's return was greeted as you can imagine. The rejoicings became the talk of the whole Mediterranean. Telemachus made Eucharis and Calypso so happy that they lost all feelings of jealousy for one another and calmly shared their lover's bed. They often met there without resentment; moreover, when Telemachus demanded a respite, they were not above reciprocating services which they found so much to their liking that they gradually managed to do without the son of Ulysses, and one fine day they advised their importunate lover to make himself scarce. Telemachus smiled coarsely and said to

Eucharis: "That is hardly like you"; and then to Calypso: "I expected no less on your part." After which, he went to see Mentor who was putting the final touches to his ship. Mentor was triumphant:

"So, what did I tell you?

— If you think I can remember, after all this time!

— Memory, this word designates the faculty of recalling the ideas and the notion of objects productive of sensation as well as the action, the effect of that faculty: memories: I remember well or I remember a mausoleum in the country (my example is a play of mirrors). Of these two meanings, the first is literal and the other can be derived figuratively. But in which of the two do we find metonymy? Just guess: you need only slap the hand that contains the marble. Chance. I cannot consider the fate of a word with indifference. Doesn't the relationship between an object and myself alter in going through the years? There is much to be learned by focusing on words that depend upon recollection. *Refresh (freshen up)* can apply to both memory and hair.[5] *Within the memory of man* is used only in negative sentences. *A reminder*[6] carries over whatever has no effect on the bottom line: each

5. An untranslatable play on words: *rafraichir* can mean refresh as well as freshen up. [Translator's note.]

6. *Pour mémoire,* literally, for memory, designates in the language of accountants sums mentioned for the sake of information but not included in the bill: a reminder. [Translator's note.]

use of a word increases the part of arbitrariness which presided at its choice. The fragile construct of chosen phonemes would collapse if we did not take it at face value: we believe, astride a heap of words, that they facilitate tangible progress. We have of the world a verbal representation, a spot of abstraction for rainy days.

— Will this lead you very far?

— To Ithaca, answered Mentor, pretending to speak of the ship.

A beribboned cow, Misochronopoulos's wet-nurse brought along her charge in her handbag. Telemachus frowned:

— There now, exclaimed Mentor, what about the bowels of fatherhood? The call of blood?

— Your jests, my dear Mentor, charm me less and less. I detest rats, toads, and other cufflinks, and that's that.

— You detest above all your memories, Telemachus, and other people's children would seem less hateful to you.

— Just because nobody ventures on their behalf to saddle me with absurdly illusory obligations. Otherwise, I would relish breaking some of them.

— Just because? But here pleasure is intensified by peering into a childish mirror, Eucharis's present. It's undoubtedly you, but redder, greasier, more slippery. A pretty likeness without hair.

— Leave me alone.

— Oh! oh! Don't get angry. Sweet Miso frowns just like you. Suck your thumb.

— Eh? what an idiot I am!

— Striking, striking. The same gesture! Finding oneself, how delightful!

— Do you expect to go on pestering me with this revolting spectacle? You who speak of memory with such self-satisfaction, tell me if it affords you endless pleasures in heredity, that other inbite of matter. A coffee mill of my sorts dislikes caricature. Hand me Miso, nurse."

Miso was tossed into the air so quickly that the nurse did not have time to tear off her horns. Swinging above the sea, he crashed out of sight so as not to soil the landscape. It is reported that Jupiter changed the victim into a cloud, but nobody knows for sure.

— If such is your opinion on the matter of inheritance, said Mentor, I hardly believe that you can lay claim to the crown of Ithaca. And Ulysses?

— My poor friend, haven't you gone beyond all that? Let's have a drink."

Ridiculous peripeteia, invented stories crowd the windows and laughably crush their noses against the panes. All the same, what a lack of imagination! When you are tired of making love, you go for a drink. When you're tired of drinking, you drink. Do you know Mr. Chériau, the building contractor? Neither do I. The door on the right leads to the phone, the door on the left to another idea. We spend our time taking the wrong street. The talk we hear assumes proportions, how should I put it? that are disproportionate. The tongue won't countenance the infamous use of language: it is made for a more noble destiny. Let us bemoan the state of servitude where we have progressively fallen in the last few years. Servitude, my dear, with your fried fish eyes, servitude, my dear girl, with your fried fish eyes. I'm getting lost, I bend under atmospheric pressure. I do very well as a manometer. I just open my mouth. Baaa. I swear that I don't feel like laughing. Life is a sad little nanny goat. Please, do not jest all the time, you make tears come to my eyes. Just like that, without motive: I don't know what's the matter with me today. My friends, what do you want to become? masons, painters of great talent; conjurers, men of the world; braggarts. Well then, in earnest! You can't start the game over again. Let's close our eyes. Nothing worse can happen to us than that something should happen which . . . The shortest distance from one point to the next, a problem of no interest. Geometrical loci, also, cause mankind considerable torment. You cannot conclude that this proves their intelligence. Please understand. Wearing earrings is a custom on the way out. What a pity! All that is left is to play heads or tails for our life. Tails, we kill ourselves, Heads, we live. Up you go!

Heads, I lose.

BOOK VII

Montes exultaverunt ut arietes
et coles sicut agni ovium.

The mountains skipped like rams,
and like lambs, the hills.

PSALM 114

On the pinkish sand, dust of prickly nacres, Telemachus and Nestor, stupefied by the heat, looked at the sea as at an old acquaintance. A slightly godlike lobster emerged and bowed before them. He handed Telemachus an alga on which was inscribed:

A CHARMING SURPRISE

I AM A DEAF MUTE

THIS SALE IS MY ONLY MEANS OF EXISTENCE

PRICE: Whatever you please.

Telemachus threw some change to the lobster which became a beautiful young woman and ran off toward the mountain. Having unfolded the seaweed, the son of Ulysses proffered it to Mentor, and, too exhausted to do it himself, asked his companion to read him what he found there. Mentor obliged:

"THE NARCISSUS: blooms under the tenth sign of the Zodiac. Its white and yellow colors, united together, divide in the following way: *white*, love of oneself; *yellow*, egoism; *flower*, passion.

"THE SUN: according to mythology was the son of Hyperion and Tria. It symbolizes fecundity and vital warmth. Its influence bodes well for people born during this fortunate month.

— Is that all?

— No, there's more on the other side: THE NARCISSUS. THE CAPRICORN: under this vivifying planet, someone in whom you had placed the utmost trust betrayed you. The great promises that were made you have not been kept. The sun in vivifying nature brings happiness to those who are born under its sign. You must fear the trickery of one of your most curious neighbors and the wickedness of someone close to you.

— Is that all?

— That's all.

What do we know of the *l'avenir*,[7] a noun that des-

7. *Avenir*, from *à venir*, meaning (events) to come, is used far more frequently to designate the future than the synonymous *futur* or

ignates future time, what must happen in that time, posterity our destiny (In the future, may an eternal silence hide this memory, Racine),[8] prosperity, success? Mentor, are you acquainted with those automatic contrivances that for a copper coin predicts a person's future? A couple stopped in front of one of those boxes. The man murmured imperishable words into the blissful ears of his companion. The woman snuggled against him and squeezed his sinewy hand. Their glances met, softly struggled, and fell on the divining contraption. They smiled. Slight noddings of the chin indicated that they were jesting with considerable emotion at the prospect of their future together. Then the man went through his pockets and put two coins in the slot. With a clanking rattle, the machine set itself in motion. Two heads bent over, and the man read while pretending to laugh:

> You have become absorbed
> in your passion
> It's time for a change.

They went off in a hurry, and after a few steps, the woman suddenly uttered a terrible cry akin to lost happiness.

---

temps futur. We might accuse Telemachus of tautological quibbling. [Translator's note.]

8. From Racine's *Phèdre*, I, iii, ever so slightly misquoted in Aragon's text. [Translator's note.]

— Eclipses discourage us from scoffing at predictions, a word that can be used in both an active and a passive sense. Divination is more usual than you might expect: we have hardly any other thought processes. All discoveries boil down to charades or predictions. The inventor of the hourglass predicted, foretold the use that would be made of it, etc. The mind, so it would seem, can take into account all conjectures, the number of which in specific cases does not exceed a figure within the limits of our powers of representation. "I give you a hundred guesses" already sounds like hyperbole. Nothing is more pleasant, more instinctive than the denial of chance.

— In some dice games, they call certain fixed points always favorable to the player holding the dice. That's why I believe in chance.

— There is no chance.

— We can state: by chance, there is no chance.

— You have pushed the difficulty one step further back. Diviners are very precisely people who know what they are talking about. Dangers are also called hazards.[9]

— Very few words cut only one way. It is generally said that in games of chance voluntary combinations play no part. Nothing could be closer to the truth or further from it. For instance: life.

9. *Hasard*, from an Arabic word referring to dice, means chance or luck as well as hazard. [Translator's note.]

— It is because there is no chance that we can know life in advance.

— I, the malice aforethought of destiny, definitely feel that I hold within my reach the power to upset the very designs of fate. If only I set my mind to it. And to what extent isn't my will itself a chance, that I should thus feel free to consider it in oposition to my destiny?

— Three cheers, young man.

— Why do you laugh?

— Little by little you are becoming like everybody else. Through tremendous efforts, you have returned to ordinary ideas. You could hardly ruin yourself more effectively. It's a fairly delightful show.

— You horrid old man, stop provoking me!

— Youth reproaches old age with reproaching it its youth. It reminds me of a snake biting its tail. But have no fears: I won't discourage you from building your own pet solar system. Catch two or three reliable certainties— a disease that is no worse than any other. So we leave tomorrow for Ithaca?

— Is that so? Have you finished your nut shell? I'm not coming with you.

— Is it Eucharis who is holding you back or Calypso?

— You won't be making fun of me much longer . . .

— There, there, don't get up: it's too hot. What secret attractions does Ogygia possess that you should prefer it to Ithaca?

— That of not being my country: since nothing ties me to the place, I'll remain.

— Hm! an obligation carried to the second power: what a predestination, this belief in your freedom!

— Mentor, you are going down hill. You do well to return to Ithaca; its unhealthy climate will deal you the final blow. Good luck.

— How subtle your irony, Telemachus, and how tasteful your words! I assure you that I am taking note of your asininity with the most extraordinary glee.

— Your wisdom within me turns against you.

— You are indeed the product of my wisdom: a nice paroxysm that has failed. You must resign yourself to having been a mere experiment. A proof too. *Reductio ad absurdum;* it's no concern of yours to know of what. Since I have insufficient knowledge of my field, Telemachuses help me get things right.

— Miserable imposter, because you feel worn out you believe that you can sidetrack me by pretending to be a great man. Just look at the folds on your stomach. Mediocre Mentor!

— So it has come to pity. What a titilating puppet! My little Telemachus, believe me, you are no more than a sentimental mistake.

— I am Telemachus, a man: a free movement set loose on earth, with power to come and go.

— I'll be damned if you don't sound just like a billiard ball.

— You make me laugh with your blackboard calculations and your bogus experiments. I'd like to know what power you ever held over me. In the world, since being myself, I walk a master. By closing my eyes I impose the night. With my steps I make life, by my absence, emptiness. Light is my possession. If I happen to forget you, you are dead.

— Just try.

— I can wander beyond your consciousness. There are marvelous zones that belong to me alone: there begin those crystals, those burning snow flowers among which I lose myself at the helm. Those regions where palm trees wear women's scarves are colonies of my body. My delight, daughter of my power, does not look like anyone else's: speak, Madam, and tell what you know (but those who once have contemplated divinity in all its majesty never desist from a general quaver during the rest of their life).

— Obviously, you know very little.

— You are inept, Mentor, just like the judgments we pass on ourselves.

— You are becoming observant: the inopportune nature of thought has just dawned on you. The fits and starts of language most adequately express your state of mind.

— Essential problems, you senile baldpate, make it blink like suns.

The essential is perhaps what exalts you?

— No: what exalts me is the essential.

— Then we agree. We would be wrongheaded if we did not take words literally. A slip is never really a slip. Words do not fail[10] us as long as they do not betray us: misnomers clearly reveal our hidden thoughts.

— All of this is totally lacking in interest: I would willingly drink chilled beverages through the bitter and yellow stems of harvests. Straws of life, straws, sweet straws, o life as refreshing as useless remorse. O for a drink.

— Hey! free man, show some obedience to the heat.

— Mentor, I look upon you with pity, for I have the wherewithal, as undoubtedly as two plus two equals four, to put an immediate stop to your jesting.

— I'm curious to test the efficacy of your little secret.

— Are you in earnest, Mentor?

— I am.

— Then you are really and truly in earnest. Well, if you must insist, Mentor, here goes."

Telemachus stood on the edge of the cliff; his clothing dropped; the naked body, young and healthy, suddenly dashed into the void, whirled, a mortal winged projectile, whirled before it crashed, a bag of broken bones, on the rocks, in front of the waves that did not even sob. Mentor

10. *Trahir* can mean fail, insofar as words fail to express our thoughts, or betray, in the sense that our words can reveal more than we intended. [Translator's note.]

moved toward the crack in the earth and shouted more loudly than the sea:

"Telemachus, the son of Ulysses, has died a fool's death to display his freedom; and his death, determined by sarcasms and gravity, is the denial of that chance which he wished to uphold at the price of his life. With Telemachus chance has perished. Now begins the reign of wisdom."

No sooner had he finished his speech than a tottering rock broke from the top of the slope and crushed, like an ordinary mortal, the goddess Minerva who had so playfully assumed the shape of an old man and who, thanks to this whim, managed to lose at the same moment her human and her divine existence. Sneering birds flew above the bodies, whistling dance tunes. Winds rose out of joy and combed their hair with the teeth of mountains. Delivered at last, forests flowed down to the dwellings of man and ate them. Stones exploded. Plants flew unconcernedly as though they had done nothing else during their entire existence. Wakened volcanoes peered at each other above the oceans, advanced toward one another and conjoined in lava loves under the kisses of craters as beneficient as rain. Waters were no longer united and coherent, but dissipated throughout the universe. The sky, a delirirous tissue torn asunder, revealed the wanton nudity of the planets.

The firmament was constellated with genitals of lights. The vault of days and nights became flesh; and those people who had survived the upheaval died of desire before the lewd rump suspended above their heads. The desert sand, changing into a snake, opened its eyes, a jolt of lightning, to the shudder of nocturnal pollutions. Nebulæ prowled among smiling landscapes. Distaffs danced while shedding their silvery locks. Great rotary presses copulated on the pebbled beaches. Jackhammers strolled prettily in the squares, and while metals, howling in the plains of pleasure, petted one another, the Lord our God astride his steeds of tenderness burst into wild guffaws.